Copyright © September 2024 Jill A. Woolford
All rights reserved. This document is geared towards providing exact and reliable information with regard to the topic and issue covered. The publication is sold with the idea that the publisher is not required to render accounting, officially permitted, or otherwise, qualified services. If advice is necessary, legal or professional, a practiced individual in the profession should be ordered.

No part of this publication may be reproduced, duplicated, distributed, or transmitted in any form or by any means, including photocopying, recording, or other electronic or mechanical methods, without the prior written permission of the publisher, except in the case of brief quotations embodied in critical reviews and certain other noncommercial uses permitted by copyright law. Recording of this publication is strictly prohibited and any storage of this document is not allowed unless with written permission from the publisher. All rights reserved.

The information provided herein is stated to be truthful and consistent, in that any liability, in terms of inattention or otherwise, by any usage or abuse of any policies, processes, or directions contained within is the solitary and utter responsibility of the recipient reader. Under no circumstances will any legal responsibility or blame be held against the publisher for any reparation, damages, or monetary loss due to the information herein, either directly or indirectly.

Respective authors own all copyrights not held by the publisher.

Printed by Kiyanni B., Write It Out Publishing, LLC. in the United States of America.
Write It Out Publishing LLC
Virginia Beach, Virginia
Writeitoutpublishing.com

ISBN: 979-8-9893223-7-4
Book Cover Illustrator: Maurice Rogers
Editor: Tamira Butler - Likely, Renee Johnson

First printing, (e-book or paperback) September 2024
Jill A. Woolford
Trenton, New Jersey
JohnThreeSixteenMin@gmail.com

KINGDOM COVENANT

The Most Expensive Engagement Ring....the Cross

Write It Out
PUBLISHING, LLC

VIRGINIA BEACH, VA

KINGDOM COVENANT

The Most Expensive Engagement Ring….the Cross

Jill A. Woolford

INTRODUCTION

Are we (The Church) dating Jesus?

I have listened to well-intentioned relationship advisers give advice on dating and how to know if that person is "the one."

I have yet to find "dating" in God's Word.

Did Adam and Eve date?

Did Isaac and Rebekah date?

So, is Jesus and the Church dating?

Let us seek clarity by the One who created marriage and the purpose of marriage. There's purpose and destiny in everything God does and creates.

Let us take this journey together, if you will.

This book will walk you through and give you a greater understanding of why **God Created Marriage** (Adam and Eve – foreshadowing of Jesus and the Church); We are to prepare to reign with our Bridegroom. As the song says, "This is just a rehearsal." **Purpose** (Why did God create Marriage?) We are responsible for bringing God's Kingdom into the earth as it was with the Garden of Eden; **Husband** (Who is he? What is his purpose?) He is to be the Priest of the home; **Wife** (Who is she? What is her purpose?) She represents the Church, the Bride of Christ; **Husband and Wife** (Who are they? What is their purpose?) They are to rule and reign together. God gave Man dominion in the earth. It's time to take dominion and walk in our dominion. **Proverbs 31** (Virtuous Woman) The description of this woman was written nearly 3000 years ago, yet the woman has been suppressed; **Consecrate For Covenant** (We Consecrate for Ministry. Why not for marriage? Is marriage not a ministry?) We are to be set apart and focus on preparation for Kingdom Covenant; and **Conversations with My Husband** (Who has God called, chosen, and graced you to be in Covenant with?) Learn of him. The same goes for husbands. Learn of your wife.

The Lord God is bringing His Kingdom sons and daughters together in Kingdom Covenant to show the world this is how His Kingdom functions through Kingdom Covenant.

Marriage has become worldly. It has become about the dress, destination (where to honeymoon), how many guests, and who to invite.

Is God invited?

Has God been invited?

Did you leave God at the altar?

DEDICATIONS

To Jesus, My Bridegroom,

Thank You for Your sacrificial, unconditional, intentional, purposeful, on-purpose love for me. Thank You for covering me, interceding for me. Thank You for choosing me. I look forward to reigning with You, my King.

There aren't enough words to explain how I feel about You.

I am so in love with You. You're beautiful.

Your Bride,

Jill

To My Husband,

I cannot wait to serve you and with you, to be at your side. Together, we will reign in the earth in harmony. We shall take territory and have dominion for the Kingdom, in Jesus name.

I cannot wait to love you.

Your wife,

Jill

Chapter 1 | God Created Marriage   **Page 15**
Adam and Eve – foreshadowing of Jesus and the Church

Chapter 2 | Purpose   **Page 51**
Why did God create Marriage?

Chapter 3 | Husband   **Page 57**
Who is he? What is his purpose?

Chapter 4 | Wife   **Page 83**
Who is she? What is her purpose?

Chapter 5 | Husband and Wife   **Page 113**
What is their purpose? Who are they?

Chapter 6 | Proverbs 31   **Page 145**

Chapter 7 | Consecrate For Covenant   **Page 155**
We Consecrate for Ministry. Why not for marriage?
Is marriage not a ministry?

Chapter 8 | Conversations with My Husband   **Page 177**

God Created Marriage

Adam and Eve – foreshadowing of Jesus and the Church

Chapter 1

Because of a tree, Man fell into sin and was separated from God

Because of a tree, Man was redeemed, sin nailed to a tree

Genesis – The Beginning

God created the heavens and the earth and founded it upon the seas. God placed the great light that rules by day and a lesser light that would rule the night; the stars in the heavens. God separated the day from the night. Then God created the fish of the seas and the fowl of the air and told them to be fruitful and multiply and fill the seas and the earth.

On the sixth day:

Creation of Man

1:26 God said, Let us make man in our image, after our likeness: and let them have dominion over the fish of the sea, and over the fowl of the air, over the cattle, and over all the earth, and over every creeping thing that creepeth upon the earth

1:27 So God created man in His own image, in the image of God created He him; male and female created He them

1:28 And God blessed them, and God said unto them, Be fruitful, and multiply, and replenish the earth, and subdue it; and have dominion over the fish of the sea, and over the follow of the air, and over every living thing that moveth upon the earth

1:29 And God said, Behold, I have given you every herb bearing seed, which is upon the face of all the earth, and every tree, in which is the fruit of a tree yielding seed; to you it shall be for meat

2:7 And the Lord God formed man of the dust of the ground, and breathed into his nostrils the breath of life; and man became a living soul

2:8 And the Lord God planted a garden eastward of Eden; and there he put the man whom he had formed

2:15 And the Lord God took the man, and put him into the garden of Eden to dress it and to keep it

2:16 And the Lord God commanded the man, saying, Of every tree of the garden thou mayest freely eat

2:17 But of the tree of the knowledge of good and evil, thou shalt not eat of it: for in the day that thou eatest thereof thou shalt sure die

2:18 And the Lord God said, it is not good that the man should be alone; I will make him an help meet for him

2:19 And out of the ground the Lord God formed every beast of the field, and every fowl of the air; and brought them unto Adam to see what he would call them; and whatsoever Adam called every living creature, that was the name thereof

2:20 And Adam gave names to all cattle, and to the fowl of the air; and to every beast of the field; but for Adam there was not found an help meet for him.

2:21 the Lord God caused a deep sleep to fall upon Adam, and he slept; and He took one of his ribs, and closed up the flesh; the rib, which the Lord God had taken from Man, made He a woman, and brought her unto the Man

2:22 And the rib, which The Lord God had taken from man, made he a woman, and brought her unto the man

2:23 Adam said this is now bone of my bones, and flesh of my flesh; she shall be called Woman because she came out of man

2:24 Therefore shall a man leave his father and mother, and shall cleave unto his wife: and they shall be one flesh

2:25 And they were both naked; the man and his wife; and were not ashamed.

When God reached into the earth, as we would like to envision, and formed Man (Adam), and breathed the breath of life into Man and Man became a living soul.

Male and female were one. Thus, when God put the man Adam to sleep to remove a rib to create woman, then present this creature to the man; who then declares, "bone of my bones, flesh of my flesh; you shall be called woman because you came out of man." Therefore, shall a wife cause a man to leave his father and mother and cleave to his wife; and the two shall become one.

The man did not recognize himself amongst the creatures God made and brought to him to name. They were more like pets. Thus, when God took the female (woman) out of the male (man), the man recognized himself in her; what God took out of, removed from him; that's why he was able to declare, "Bone of my bones, flesh of my flesh; I shall call you woman because you came out of man."

Genesis 3

1 Now the serpent was more subtil than any beast of the field which the Lord God made. And he said unto the woman, Yeah, hath God said, Ye shall not eat of every tree of the garden?

2 And the woman said unto the serpent, We may eat of the fruit of the trees of the garden:

3 But of the fruit of the tree which is in the midst of the garden, God hath said, Ye shall not eat of it, neither shall ye touch it, lest ye die.

4 And the serpent said unto the woman, Ye shall not surely die.

5 For God doth know that in the day ye eat thereof then your eyes shall be opened, and ye shall be as gods, knowing good and evil

6 And when the woman saw that the tree was good for food, and that it was pleasant to the eyes, and the tree to be desired to make one wise, she took of the fruit thereof, and did eat, and gave also unto her husband with her; and he did it

7 And the eyes of them both were opened, and they knew that they were naked; and they sewed fig leaves together; and made themselves aprons

8 And they heard the voice of the Lord God walking in the garden in the cool of the day: and Adam and his wife hid themselves from the presence of the Lord God amongst the trees of the garden

12 And the man said, The woman whom thou gavest me to be with me, she gave me of the tree, and I did eat

13 And the Lord God said unto the woman, What is this that thou hast done?

And the woman said, The serpent beguiled me, and I did eat

Adam and Eve were a foreshadowing of the Bridegroom and the Church. They were already Kings in the earth, Lords in the earth. Satan recognized God's Kingdom in the earth because that's where he once lived in the Heavens; until he decided he wanted to rule and reign in God's Kingdom.

When God found the iniquity in Lucifer's heart, he was swiftly thrown out of Heaven. (Isaiah 14:12 Ezekiel 28:14-16)

Jesus said, I saw Satan fall like lightning to the earth. (Luke 10:18)

Satan beguiled the Woman with the same tricks he uses today; lust of the eyes, lust of the flesh, and the pride of life. Why did Satan approach the woman?

Did Satan think the woman was the weaker vessel?

Satan went after the favor of God when he approached the wife. The husband did not protect his wife, did not guard the *ezer* (favor) God gave him; yet he blamed God.

Just as Satan went after the woman, Satan has been attacking the Church, the Bride of Christ, the woman. Lucifer wanted to rise to the most High God's throne and be like the Most High God. He thought because of his beauty that he deserved to be worshipped.

Christ Jesus is called the last Adam and the Body of Christ, the Church, His Bride.

The first man Adam blamed God for the woman. The last man Adam went to the cross to restore what was lost, stolen in the garden; to restore the woman, who is the Bride of Christ. Kingship. Lordship. They hung Him high, stretched Him wide; He hung His head, then He died; then the soldier pierced His side, forthwith came there out blood and water to purify and redeem His Bride. (see John 19:34) The first man Adam disobeyed God and gave dominion to Satan. The last man Adam took it back when He went to the cross. He rose with all power with the keys to death and hell.

When man disobeys God, man gives Satan access, dominion over his life.

O death where is your sting; O grave where is your victory?

The first man Adam did not restore and probably couldn't because he sinned by eating the fruit; giving into temptation. The last man Adam (Jesus) was tempted at all points, but did not sin. He became sin for us, a propitiation, a substitute. The last man Adam was without sin and was hung on a tree to become sin for us. Without the shedding of blood, there cannot be remission of sin. The first bloodshed to cover sin was in the garden of Eden when God sacrificed animals and used their skins to cover Adam and his wife. Before that, they were naked and unashamed, covered in God's glory. Once their eyes were opened, after eating of the fruit of the knowledge of good and evil, they became ashamed of their nakedness. That's what sin does. Then God covered their sin with the blood sacrifice of animals. Jesus, the Lamb of God, sacrificed once and for all.

Kingdom Covenant expressed by a marriage: the responsibility of the wife and the responsibility of the husband.

Ephesians 5:22-33

> 22 Wives, submit yourselves unto your own husbands, as unto the Lord
>
> 23 For the husband is the head of the wife, even as Christ is the head of the church: and he is the savior of the body
>
> 24 Therefore as the church is subject unto Christ, so let the wives be to their own husbands in everything.
>
> 25 Husbands, love your wives, even as Christ also loved the church, and gave himself for it.
>
> 26 That he might sanctify and cleanse it with the washing of water by the word,
>
> 27 That he might present it to himself a glorious church, not having spot, or wrinkle, or any such thing; but that it should be holy and without blemish.
>
> 28 So ought men to love their wives as their own bodies. He that loveth his wife loveth himself.
>
> 29 For no man ever yet hated his own flesh; but nourisheth and cherisheth it, even as the Lord the church:

30 For we are members of his body, of his flesh, and of his bones.

31 For this cause shall a man leave his father and mother, and shall be joined unto his wife, and they two shall be one flesh.

32 This is a great mystery: but I speak concerning Christ and the church.

33 Nevertheless let every one of you in particular so love his wife even as himself; and the wife see that she reverence her husband.

As you can see in Ephesians 5:22-33, most of the instructions are given to the Bridegroom because it was God the Father, Son, and Holy Ghost that decided this was how Man was to be redeemed.

Revelation 19:7, Let us be glad and rejoice, and give honour to him: for the marriage of the Lamb is come, and his wife hath made herself ready.

19:8 And to her was granted that she should be arrayed in fine linen, clean and white: for the fine linen is the righteousness of saints.

19:9…Blessed are they which are called unto the marriage supper of the Lamb.

Leave thy father and mother and cleave to your wife. (Genesis 2:24; cr Matthew 19:5)

Wherefore they are no more twain (two), but one flesh. What therefore God hath joined together, let no man put asunder (Matthew 19:6)

He sent redemption unto His people: He hath commanded His covenant forever: holy and reverend is His name. (Psalm 111:9)

Jesus cried on that cross, "It is finished." What was finished? EVERYTHING.

This is Kingdom Covenant; the Bridegroom sacrificing, covering His Bride. His Bride becoming one with her Bridegroom in submission and reverence.

This is Kingdom Covenant and Kingdom Principles. The Covenant is the Cross. When God the Father, The Son, and The Holy Ghost planned for The Son to come into the earth, the Lamb slain before the foundation of the World, God knew the Cross was the only way to save and redeem mankind. Thy Kingdom come, thy will be done, in earth as it is in Heaven. Jesus brought Heaven into the earth. There is no one deaf, blind, dumb, lame, poor, sick, diseased, hungry, angry, hurt, depressed, or sad in Heaven.

Husband and wife were created to reign together in the earth. Our Father and Mother (Adam and Eve) were created to reign in the earth together. God gave Man dominion in the earth. Their disobedience gave Satan dominion. Jesus took dominion back when Satan used Man to crucify Him; crushing Satan's head.

The Cross is our engagement ring.

When Jesus said, pick up your cross and follow me, denying everyone, He was giving us an engagement ring. Jesus said, unless you forsake mother, father, brother and sister, and pick up your cross and follow me, you will not be part of the Kingdom.

Luke 14:26-27
> 26 If any man come to me, and hate not his father, and mother, and wife, and children, and brethren, and sisters, yea, and his own life also, he cannot be my disciple
>
> 27 And whosoever doth not bear his cross, and come after me, cannot be my disciple

Matthew 19:29 And every one that hath forsaken houses, or brethren, or sisters, or father, or mother, or wife, or children, or lands, for my name's sake, shall receive an hundredfold, and shall inherit everlasting life.

For where your treasure is, there your heart will be. (Matthew 6:19-21)

What do you treasure? Is it things? Earthly things? God treasures us, His children. He put treasure in earthen vessels. (2 Corinthians 4:7)

How many times have we given the engagement ring back to Jesus? How many times have we dropped our crosses?

When you and I were called out of the world, the world should have been left behind, so *DO NOT* take the concepts, systems of the world and try to blend it, marry it to the Word of God. Each of us should have divorced the world once we were called out. One cannot truly say I am born again, I am a new creature in Christ Jesus, yet try to blend, marry, if you will, the world to the Word of

God. No. Be not conformed to the world, but be ye transformed by the renewing of your mind. We are supposed to be Christ-like, have the mind, heart, and ways of Jesus.

Otherwise, you and I are committing adultery against God. Yes, you can commit adultery against God. It's not just between husband and wife. "Thou shalt not commit adultery" is one of the commandments God gave in Exodus 20:14, cr Jeremiah 3:8. You're cheating on God with Satan. Adultery is a physical and emotional abandonment.

The only time the Church discusses Kingdom Covenant (marriage) and marriage counseling, is when the man gets down on his knee and asks this specific woman to marry him and she says yes.

Covenant, Kingdom Covenant in the earth is preparation for the ultimate Kingdom Covenant between the Bridegroom and His Bride. The Church needs to be prepared for her Bridegroom. Our Bridegroom doesn't know when He is coming back. Do not run out of oil. Do not fall asleep. You'll be left behind. You must learn to bring God's Kingdom in the earth. The only way to do that is that God's Kingdom must be in each of us. In order to do that is to be born again. (John 3) Apostle Paul gives the principles for Kingdom Covenant in Ephesians Chapter 5; 1 Corinthians Chapter 13, the Apostle Paul teaches how to love.

You and I are in the process of becoming the Bride of Christ; of becoming one with Christ. The Cross is our engagement ring. It's not Jesus who keeps taking the Cross (the engagement ring) back. It's Man whenever we sin; whether it is by disobedience, fornication, adultery, pride, arrogance, causing strife, division, etc. It is Man that leaves Jesus at the altar. It is Man that breaks the engagement over and over again.

Naked and unashamed with the Bridegroom

This is spiritual. Yes, He knows everything, yet He wants you to be able to be open with Him; to have an intimate relationship with Him where you can tell your deepest secrets, deepest hurts, deepest desires and be unashamed.

In Christ Jesus, there is no more condemnation. (Romans 8:1)

Our Bridegroom sacrificed Himself for us, me, you. Now that's love – sacrificial, unconditional, intentional, on purpose, purposeful.

Love one another as I have loved you. (John 13:34)

May they be as one, as the Father and I are one. (John 17:21)

The Church is Jesus' rib.

Jesus' side was pierced and out came water and blood to purify and redeem Man; so that His Bride will be presented to Him without spot, wrinkle, or blemish. Holy. Romans 12:1, present your bodies as a living sacrifice; holy, acceptable unto God, which is your (our) reasonable service. Know ye not that your body is the temple of the Holy Ghost, which is in you. (see 1 Corinthians 6:19)

And the two shall become one. Jesus will declare, "Bone of my bones, flesh of my flesh" at the marriage supper of the Lamb. (see Revelations 19:17-19) Essentially, our heavenly Father is our Father-in-love.

It is the Word of God that washes us clean. It is the Blood of Jesus that redeems. Jesus is the Word of God.

The main purpose of Kingdom Covenant is to teach us to reign in the earth in preparation to reign with Christ Jesus. Our Father chooses the Bride for His Son. Our Father chose Jesus' disciples. (John 17:9)

God has been trying to equip His Church for spiritual warfare and for the marriage supper to reign with her Bridegroom, His Son.

How can we reign with Jesus when we do not know how to reign in the earth?

Reigning is about order, justice, peace, love, joy, charity, prosperity.

The second most important thing, which accompanies the first, is to bring God's Kingdom into the earth through Kingdom Covenant – Marriage. The garden of Eden was God's Kingdom in the earth.

God is a God of order, not chaos, not confusion

God is a God of love, not evil, not hate

God is a God of peace, not war

God is a God of joy, not depression

God is a God of charity, not selfishness

God is a God of longsuffering (patience), not I gotta have it now

God is a God of temperance (self-control), not undisciplined

God is a God of meekness, not power hungry

God is a God of faith, not flakiness, non-dependable.

God's love is sacrificial, unconditional, intentional, on-purpose, purposeful. (John 3:16)

This is all about Restoration; has always been about Restoration. Satan knows if we knew who we were, are, in the earth, his days in the earth would be shorter. Satan should have been in the lake of fire. The Church is delaying the return of Jesus.

When Satan sees marriage, especially a true Kingdom Covenant, he will find a way, just as he did in the garden of Eden. He found a serpent willing to be used. After that, he has been using two-legged serpents, Man.

This is all about Genesis 1:26; God giving Man dominion in the earth. Satan wanted to reign in Heaven, then saw an opportunity with the garden of Eden, which was Heaven in the earth. God's Kingdom in the earth. Then, Satan found an ally in a serpent.

We are to model to our families, to the World, what God's Kingdom looks like.

Keep in mind, we are Spirit wrapped in flesh, having a human experience. We are spiritual beings housed in a tabernacle, a temple.

What we do in the earth is all preparation to reign with Christ Jesus. How can we reign with Christ Jesus if we do not learn to reign as the body of Christ?

God is commanding us to take our rightful place in the earth. He gave Man dominion from the beginning.

As the Bride of Christ, we took His name and are called Christians. Christ means,

"Holy anointed One." We are to be Holy, Anointed Ones.

The Apostle Peter said it like this (1 Peter 2:9), But ye are:

A Chosen Generation

A Royal Priesthood

A Holy Nation

A peculiar people (uncommon, unusual, distinctive)

That you should shew forth praises of him who hath called you out of darkness into his marvelous light

As the Bride of Christ, we are covered under His name. Jesus said, Verily, verily, I say unto you, Whatsoever ye shall ask the Father in my name, he will give it you. (John 16:23)

Sometimes, we must go back to the beginning and re-read and understand the instructions God gave us. We must know and understand who we are in God and in the earth. We are Kings. Jesus is the King of Kings. We are Lords. Jesus is the Lord of Lords. Satan challenged Man's identity, Adam. God established our identity and our authority in Genesis 1:26-28. We were gods in the earth from the beginning when God created Man (Adam).

After Jesus was baptized, He was led into the wilderness by the Holy Spirit to be tempted of Satan. After fasting 40 days and 40 nights, the first thing Satan did was question Jesus about His identity; if you are the son of God…(Matt 4:1-11).

Jesus sent the Holy Ghost to walk with us, to talk with us; just as He did with our Father and Mother in the garden of Eden.

Jesus had to be baptized because: (1) He was born into a fallen, sinful world; and (2) to show us the way, how to use the word of God against temptation.

The Apostle Paul said he had to die to his flesh daily. (1 Corinthians 15:31)

Romans 6:3-8, 3 Know ye not, that so many of us as were baptized into Jesus Christ were baptized into his death? 4 Therefore we are buried with Him by baptism unto death: that like as Christ was raised up from the dead by the glory of the Father, even so we also should walk in newness of life. 5 For if we have been planted together in the likeness of his death, we shall be also in the likeness of His resurrection; 6 Knowing this, that our old man is crucified with Him, that the body of sin might be destroyed, that henceforth we should not serve sin 7 for he that is dead is freed from sin. 8 Now if we be dead with Christ, we believe that we shall also live with Him.

And He said to them all, If any man shall come after me, let him deny himself; and take up his cross daily, and follow me (Luke 9:23)

Watch and pray, lest you fall into temptation. (Mark 14:38; Matth. 26:41)

Not my will be done; thy will be done. (Luke 22:42; Matth. 6:9-10)

The son of man didn't want to go to the cross. The Son of God chose to go to the cross.

Have you picked up your cross to follow Jesus?

The Church is God's government in the earth. We are supposed to be ruling, not the world. Yet, the world has dominion in the earth. Although Jesus rose with all power in His hands, as His Bride, we have access to the power by speaking, "In the name of Jesus."

On this rock I shall build my Church

Matthew 16:15 He saith unto them, But whom say ye that I am?

16 And Simon Peter answered and said, Thou art the Christ, the Son of the living God.

17 Jesus answered and said unto him, Blessed art thou, Simon Bar Jona: for flesh and blood hath not revealed it unto thee, but my Father which is in Heaven.

18 And I say also unto thee, That thou art Peter, and upon this rock I will build my church; and the gates of hell shall not prevail against it.

19 And I will give unto thee the keys of the kingdom of heaven: and whatsoever thou shall bind on earth shall be bound in heaven; and whatsoever thou shall loose on earth shall be loosed in heaven.

The Church has never been a building. At the birth of the Church, the Church gathered in homes. The Apostles went from home to home communing with the newly converted. The Church. When this pandemic shut down the world, your home should have been your sanctuary; and should have been your sanctuary prior to the pandemic. If the Holy Ghost is in you, then He is with you wherever you are, wherever you go. Amen.

Our Father prophesied when he called our Mother, Eve. Eve means Mother of all living. The Church is supposed to be the Mother of all living.

How do we see a Mother? A Mother gathers her children close to her, protects them, feeds, nourishes, bathes/washes, clothes and teaches. She is an incubator/carrier of life, a disciplinarian. She is unconditional love, a nurse; picks you up when you fall, gives you medicine when necessary.

The Apostle Paul said it like this: we are joint heirs with Christ Jesus. (Romans 8:17)

How are we different from the Sadducees and Pharisees?

We are supposed to preach and teach the Word of God, the Gospel of Jesus Christ; not what the world says, what God says.

How can we change the world when we are no different from the world?
> Dr. Tony Evans. He said, "God is not going to the White House without stopping by His house first."

For the time is come that judgment must begin at the house of God; and it first begin at us; what shall the end be of them that obey not the gospel of God? (1 Peter 4:17)

We are the Church, Yes? We were created to reign in the earth. We were born to reign in the earth.

Revelation 5:10 And hast made us unto our God kings and priests: and we shall reign on the earth.

Revelation 11:15 And the seventh angel sounded: and there were great voices in heaven, saying, The kingdoms of this world are become the kingdoms of our Lord, and of his Christ; and he shall reign for ever and ever

Revelation 20:6 Blessed and holy is he that hath part in the first resurrection:

on such the death hath no power, but they shall be priests of God and of Christ, and shall reign with him a thousand years.

Revelation 22:5 And there shall be no night there; and they need no candle, neither light of the sun: for the Lord God giveth them light: and they shall reign for ever and ever.

Binding and Loosing

Matthew 18:15-20 15 Moreover, if thy brother shall trespass against thee, go and tell him his fault between thee and him alone: if he shall hear thee, thou hast gained a brother. 16 But if he will not hear thee, then take with thee one or two more, that in the mouth of two or three witnesses every word may be established. 17 And if he shall neglect to hear them, tell it unto the church: but if he neglect to hear the church, let him be unto thee as an heathen man and a publican. 18 Verily I say unto you, Whatsoever ye shall bind on earth shall be bound in heaven: and whatsoever ye shall loose on earth shall be loosed in heaven. 19. Again I say unto you, That if two of you shall agree on earth as touching anything that they shall ask, it shall be done for them of my Father which is in Heaven. 20. For where two or three are gathered together in my name, there am I in the midst of them.

What are you allowing or not allowing, Church?

God sees the beginning from the end. He already knows what is going to happen. That's why Jesus was the Lamb slain before the foundations of the World.

God was not surprised when our Father and Mother disobeyed Him.

John 1:29, The next day John seeth Jesus coming unto him, and saith, Behold the Lamb of God, which taketh away the sin of the world

Jesus was the Passover lamb for Man's redemption, so that death would pass over us, Man. God knew that Man would not, could not, and cannot suffer for our sin.

The law came by Moses, but grace and truth came by Jesus Christ.

Grace and truth is the person of Jesus Christ, not what he says or she says.

Jesus said in John 3 that we must be born again to see the Kingdom of God;

being baptized by water and the Holy Ghost and fire.

Water is for purification. The fire of the Holy Ghost will burn up the chaff in your soul. Old things are passed away, behold all things are new. There is no more condemnation in Christ Jesus. You are a new creature in Christ Jesus. (Romans 8:1; 2 Corinthians 5:17)

Be not conformed to this world but be transformed by the renewing of your mind. (Romans 12:2)

He that sows to the flesh shall reap eternal damnation. He that sows to the spirit shall have eternal life. (Galatians 6:8)

The flesh wars against the spirit. The spirit wars against the flesh. (Galatians 5:17; Matthew 26:41)

Are you feeding your flesh?

Galatians 5:24 And they that are Christ's have crucified the flesh with the affections and lusts 25 If we live in the Spirit, let us also walk in the Spirit 26 Let us not be desirous of vain glory, provoking one another, envying one another

Romans 7:15-22 15 For which I do I allow not: for what I would, that do I not: but what I hate, that I do. 16 If then I do that which I would not, I consent unto the law that it is good. 17 Now then it is no more I that do it, but sin that dwelleth in me. 18 For I know that in me (that is, in my flesh) dwelleth no good thing; for to will is present with me; but how to perform that which is good I find not. 19 For the good that I would I do not; but the evil which I would not, that I do. 20 Now if I do that I would not, it is no more I that do it, but sin that dwelleth in me. 21 I find then a law, that, when I would do good, evil is present with me. 22 For I delight in the law of God after the inward man.

Romans 8:13 For if ye live after the flesh, ye shall die: but if ye through the Spirit do mortify the deeds of the body, ye shall live

Philippians 4:13 I can do all things through Christ which strengtheneth me.

Jesus said ye shall know them by their fruits. (Matthew 7:15-20)

Jesus told the religious people that He was not concerned about what was going in His disciples mouths. He was worried about what was coming out of their mouths. (Matthew 15:11)

Guard your heart, for out of it flows the issues of life. (Proverbs 4:23)

The Holy Ghost will teach you the things of God. He is our Father's Spirit Jesus sent into the earth. That was prophesied by the Prophet Joel, which Apostle Peter quoted on the day of Pentecost. (Joel 2:28-30; Acts 2:17-18)

Man was walking in Heaven in the garden of Eden; where God met them at an appointed time.

The most powerful thing God gave Man is the freedom of choice.

God wants us to choose Him.

God says I put before you life and death; blessings and cursings. I'd prefer that you choose life. (Deuteronomy 30:19)

Joshua said choose who you will serve today; as for me and my house, we shall serve the Lord. (Joshua 24:15)

Psalm 1:1-6
- 1:1 Blessed is the man that walketh not in the counsel of the ungodly, nor standeth in the way of the sinners, nor sitteth in the seat of the scornful
- 1:2 But his delight is in the law of the Lord; and in his law doth he meditate day and night
- 1:3 And she shall be like a tree planted by the rivers of water, that bringeth forth his fruit in his season; his leaf also shall not wither; and whatsoever he doeth shall prosper
- 1:4 The ungodly are not so: but are like the chaff which the wind driveth away
- 1:5 Therefore the ungodly shall not stand in the judgment, nor sinners in the congregation of the righteous
- 1:6 For the Lord knoweth the way of the righteous: but the way of the ungodly shall perish.

Hebrews 1:1-3
> 1:1 God, who at sundry times and in divers manners spake in time past unto the fathers by the prophets,
>
> 1:2 Hath in these last days spoken unto us by His Son, whom He hath appointed heir of all things, by whom also He made the worlds
>
> 1:3 Who being the brightness of His glory, and the express image of His person, and upholding all things by the word of His power, when He had by Himself purged our sins, sat down on the right hand of the Majesty on high

Romans 5:14 Nevertheless death reigned from Adam to Moses, even over them that had not sinned after the similitude of Adam's transgression, who is the figure of him that was to come

Romans 5:17 For if by one man's offence death reigned by one: much more they which receive abundance of grace and of the gift of righteousness shall reign in life by one, Jesus Christ

God expects a return on His investment

"This is just a rehearsal."

Kingdom Covenant should be taught once you become a Christian, step by step. It is part of the process of being born again, the knowledge of who/whose you are. Milk, soft food, fruits, vegetables, hamburger, chuck steak, prime rib to filet mignon, if you will.

Be fruitful, multiply and fill the earth

For the kingdom of heaven is as a man travelling into a far country, who called his own servants, and delivered unto them his goods. And unto one he gave five talents, to another two, and to another one; to every man according to this several ability; and straightway took his journey. Then he that had received the five talents went and traded with the same, and made them other five talents. And likewise he that had received two, he also gained other two. But he that had received one went and digged in the earth, and hid his lord's money. After a long time, the lord of those servants cometh, and reckoneth with them. And so he that had received five talents came and brought other five talents, saying, Lord, thou deliveredst unto me five talents; behold, I have gained beside them five talents more. His lord said unto him, Well done, thou good and faithful servant: thou hast been faithful over a few things, I will make thee ruler over many things: enter thou into the joy of the lord. He also that had received two talents came and said, Lord, thou deliveredst unto me two talents; behold, I have gained two other talents beside them. His lord said unto him Well done, good and faithful servant; thou hast been faithful over a few things, I will make thee ruler over many things: enter thou into the joy of thy lord. Then he which had received the one talent came and said, Lord, I knew thee that thou art an hard man, reaping where thou has not sown, and gathering where thou hast not strawed: And I was afraid, and went and hid thy talent in the earth: lo, there thou hast that is thine. His lord answered and said unto him, Thou wicked and slothful servant, thou knewest that I reap where I sowed not, and gather where I have not strawed: Thou oughtest therefore to have put my money to the exchangers, and then at my coming I should have received mine own with usury. Take therefore the talent from him, and give it unto him which hath five talents. For unto every one that hath shall be given, and he shall have abundance; but from him that hath not shall be taken away even that which he hath. (Matthew 25:14-29 KJV)

God does not like slothful servants.

We were bought with a price; the Blood of His Son, Jesus. For ye are bought with a price. (1 Corinthians 6:20) Not slothful in business: fervent in spirit; serving the Lord. (Romans 12:11)

Proverbs 24:30-34 (Tanakh) 30 I passed by the field of a lazy man, by the vineyard of a man lacking sense. 31 It was all overgrown with thorns; its surface was covered with chickweed, and its stone fence lay in ruins. 32 I observed and took it to heart; I saw it and learned a lesson. 33 A bit more sleep, a bit more slumber, a bit more hugging yourself in bed, 34 and poverty will come calling upon you, and want, like a man with a shield.

You must be born again

John 3:3-6

> 3 Jesus answered and said unto him, Verily, verily, I say unto thee, Except a man be born again, he cannot see the kingdom of God

> 4 Nicodemus saith unto him, How can a man be born when he is old? Can

he enter the second time into his mother's womb, and be born?

5. Jesus answered, Verily, verily, I say unto thee, Except a man be born of water and of the Spirit, he cannot enter into the kingdom of God

6 That which is born of the flesh is flesh: and that which is born of the Spirit is spirit

The world we are born into is a fallen and sinful world. That's why we must be born again. You have to be born again in order to see the Kingdom of God. You must become the Bride of Christ to inherit the Kingdom of God. God will not show you the Kingdom until you become a citizen of the Kingdom.

Have you ever asked God what can you do for the Kingdom? Do for God? Now, that's purpose. Lord, here am I, what can these fragile hands do for you? How can his earthen vessel serve the Kingdom?

Isaiah 55:7-11 Let the wicked forsake his way, and the unrighteous man his thoughts; and let him return unto the Lord, and He will have mercy upon him; and to our God, for He will abundantly pardon

8 For My thoughts are not your thoughts, neither are your ways My ways, saith the Lord

9 For as the Heavens are higher than the earth, are My ways higher than your ways, and My thoughts than you thoughts

10 For as the rain cometh down, and snow from Heaven, and returneth not thither, but watereth the earth, and maketh it bring forth and bud, that it may give seed to the sower, and bread to the eater;

11 So shall my Word be that goeth forth out of My mouth; it shall not return unto Me void; but it shall accomplish that which I please, and it shall prosper in the thing whereto I sent it.

In the book of Hosea, a picture of God, Hosea had to purchase his wife to save her. Jesus is married to the backslider, to the adulterer.

In the book of the Song of Solomon, it's a picture of Jesus wooing His Church.

The Church running after the Bridegroom. Jesus is the lover of our souls. He is

the Lily of the Valley. He is the Rose of Sharon.

Come now, and let us reason together, saith the Lord (Isaiah 1:18, part a)

God is trying to restore us back to our rightful place. We are Kings in the earth. We are Lords in the earth. Take your rightful place, thus saith the Lord. Do you know who you are, Adam?

When Jesus came into the earth, it was for a purpose. He came to restore that which was lost. Kingship. Lordship. This has all been about Restoration. Kingdom Covenant is about Restoration.

Satan does not have new tricks: The lust of the eyes. The lust of the flesh. The pride of life. Satan is here to steal, kill, and destroy the seed of the Woman. Just as he used the serpent in the garden to beguile our Mother, he uses two-legged serpents today, many that are close to us or close enough to us to steal, kill, and destroy. Satan knows we have the authority to crush his head, to tear down the kingdom of darkness soul by soul. As Christians, we are in the world but not of it.

It was the Woman who was deceived by Satan who then caused her husband to disobey God. Jesus came to restore the Woman to her rightful place; and that is to reign with her husband. She cannot reign until she is restored.

The Word of God says that we are joint heirs with Christ Jesus (Romans 8). We, the Ekklesia (Church), were called out of the darkness into His glorious Light. The word Church was translated from the Greek word Ekklesia, which means to call out. The Church has been and is being called out of the world. Adam's wife was called out of him.

We fell into darkness because of our Father and Mother's disobedience. When the Light of the world came into the world, the darkness comprehended it not; couldn't do anything about the Light. (John 1:3)

There's no chaos and foolishness in Heaven. God is a God of love and order.

These things I command you, that ye love one another as I have loved you. (John 15:17-24 v. 17) Be not deceived; God is not mocked: for whatsoever a man soweth, that shall he also reap. (Galatians 6:7) If a man says, I love God, and hateth his brother, he is a liar. (1 John 4:20-21 v.20) Though I speak with the tongues of man, and of angels, and have not charity (love), I am become as a sounding brass, or a tinkling cymbal. Follow after charity (love), and desire spiritual gifts, but rather that ye may prophesy (1 Corinthians 13:1-8,13 v.1) Let all your things be done with charity (love). (1 Corinthians 16:14) If ye then be risen with Christ, seek those things which are above, where Christ sitteth, on the right hand of God. (Colossians 3 v.1)

And above all things have fervent charity among yourselves; for charity shall cover the multitude of sins. (1 Peter 4:8) Hatred stirreth up strifes, but love covereth all sins (Proverbs 10:12) Use hospitality one to another without grudging (1 Peter 4:9-14 v.9)

But now hath God set the members every one of them in the body, as it hath pleased Him (1 Corinthians 12:18)

Psalm 8

  1 O Lord our Lord, how excellent is thy name in all the earth! Who hast set thy glory above the Heavens.

  2 Out of the mouth of babes and sucklings hast thou ordained strength because of thine enemies, that thou mightest still the enemy and the avenger. (cr Psalm 44:16; 1 Corinthians 1:27)

  3 When I consider thy heavens, the work of thy fingers, the moon, and the stars, which thou hast ordained,

  4 What is man that thou art mindful of him? and the son of man, that thou visiteth him?

  5 For thou hast made him a little lower than the angels, and hast crowned him with glory and honor.

  6 Thou hast made him to have dominion over the works of thy hands, thou hast put all things under his feet.

  7 All the sheep and oxen, yea, and the beasts of the field;

  8 The fowl of the air, and the fish of the sea, and whatsoever passeth through the paths of the seas.

  9 O Lord, our Lord, how excellent is thy name in all the earth!

Romans 8

1 There is therefore now no more condemnation to them which are in Christ Jesus, who walk not after the flesh, but after the Spirit

2 For the law of the Spirit of life in Christ Jesus hath made me free from the law of sin and death.

3 For what the law could not do, in that it was weak through the flesh, God sending His own Son in the likeness of sinful flesh, and for sin, condemned sin in the flesh.

15 For ye have not received the spirit of bondage again to fear; but ye have received the Spirit of adoption, whereby we cry, Abba, Father.

16 The Spirit itself bearest witness with our spirit, that we are the children of God:

17 And if children, then heirs of God, and joint-heirs with Christ; if so be that we suffer with him, that we may be also glorified together.

18 For I reckon that the sufferings of this present time are not worthy to be compared with the glory which shall be revealed in us.

19 For the earnest expectation of the creature waiteth for the manifestation of the sons of God.

20 For the creature was made subject to vanity, not willingly, but by reason of him who hath subjected the same in hope,

21 Because the creature itself also shall be delivered from the bondage of corruption into the glorious liberty of the children of God.

22 For we know the that the whole creation groaneth and travaileth in pain together until now

23 And not only they, but ourselves also, which have the firstfruits of the Spirit, even we ourselves groan within ourselves, waiting for the adoption, to wit, the redemption of our body.

The Tabernacle (Tent of Meetings) was when and where the cross first appeared. God commanded the Israelites through Moses to build a Tabernacle.

Chapter 1 | God Created Marriage

The Tribes encamped about the Tabernacle based on the size of the Tribes.

Exodus 25-28 Pre-incarnate crucifixion. The Cross at Calvary was the fulfillment.

The Tabernacle was covered in red-dyed animal skin, so when God looked down from Heaven, He saw the blood…on the cross.

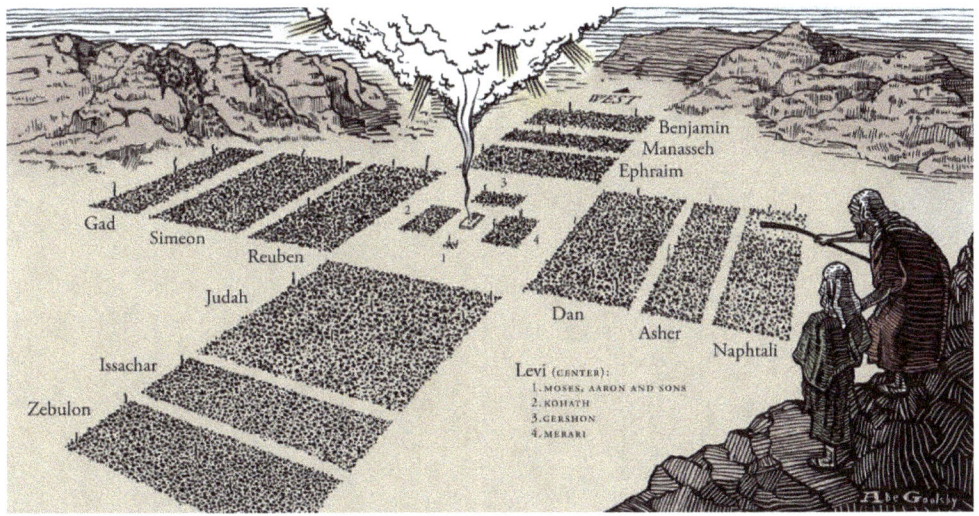

*Footnote: I happened to be tuned into the last 10 minutes of Sid Roth's It's Supernatural several years ago. His guest was a doctor/theologian and he had built a miniature of the Tabernacle and how the Israelites were encamped around the Tabernacle) The various shapes in the Tabernacle were shaped like our internal organs

The Cross The Church

Ephesians 4:4-11 (AMP) 4 There is one body {of believers] and one Spirit—just as you were called to one hope when called [to salvation] 5 one Lord, one faith, one baptism 6 one God and Father of us all who is [sovereign] overall and [working] through all and [living] in all 7 Yet grace [God's undeserved favor] was given to each one of us [not discriminately, but in different ways] in proportion to the measure of Christ's [rich and abundant] gift 8 Therefore it says, When He ascended on high, He led captivity captive, and He bestowed gifts on men; 9 (Now this expression, "He ascended," what does it mean except that He also had previously descended [from the heights of heaven] into the lower parts of the earth? 10 He who descended is the very same as He who also has ascended high above all the heavens, that He [His presence] might fill all things [that is, the whole universe]. 11 And [His gifts to the church were varied and] He Himself appointed some as apostles [special messengers, representatives], some as prophets [who speak a new message from God to the people], some as evangelists [who spread the good news of salvation], and some as pastors and teachers [to shepherd and guide and instruct].

```
                        J
                        E
                        S
                        U
                        S
APOSTLE PROPHET EVANGELIST PASTOR TEACHER
                        D
                        I
                        S
                        C
                        I
                        P
                        L
                        E
                        S
```

Ephesians 4:12-13 (AMP) 12 [and He did this] to fully equip and perfect the saints (God's people) for works of service, to build up the body of Christ [the Church] 13 until we all reach oneness in the faith and in the knowledge of the Son of God, [growing spiritually] to become a mature believer, reaching to the measure of the fullness of Christ [manifesting His spiritual completeness and exercising our spiritual gifts in unity].

1 Corinthians 12:1,4-11 (AMP) 1 Now about the spiritual gifts [the special endowments given by the Holy Spirit], brothers and sisters, I do not want you to be uninformed; 4 Now there are [distinctive] varieties of spiritual gifts [special abilities given by the grace and extraordinary power of the Holy Spirit operating in believers], but it is the same Spirit [who grants them and empowers believers] 5 And there are [distinctive] varieties of ministries and service, but it is the same Lord [who is served]. 6 And there are [distinctive] ways of working [to accomplish things], but it is the same God who produces all things in all believers [inspiring, energizing, and empowering them]. 7 But to each one is given the manifestation of the Spirit [the spiritual illumination and the enabling of the Holy Spirit] for the common good. 8 To one is given through the [Holy] Spirit [the power to speak] the message of wisdom, and to another [the power to express] the word of knowledge and understanding according to the same Spirit. 9 to another [wonder-working] faith [is given] by the same [Holy] Spirit, and to another the [extraordinary] gifts of healings by the one Spirit; 10 and to another the working of miracles, and to another prophecy [foretelling the future, speaking a new message from God to the people], and to another discernment of spirits [the ability to distinguish sound, godly doctrine from the deceptive doctrine of man-made religions and cults], to another various kinds of [unknown] tongues, and to another interpretation of tongues. 11 All these things [the gifts, the achievements, the abilities, the empowering] are brought about by one and the same [Holy] Spirit, distributing to each one individually just as He chooses.

1 Corinthians 6:2-5 v2 Do ye not know that saints shall judge the world? And if the world shall be judged by you, are ye unworthy to judge the smallest matters?

Jesus said a house divided will not stand. (Matthew 12:22-28)

As the Body of Christ, we have the responsibility to be witnesses of Christ Jesus; His redemptive blood; new creatures; born again. We all have different gifts, yet for the same purpose, witnessing.

As individuals, as a child of God, you and I are Ambassadors of Heaven, of God's Kingdom. When Jesus said pray like this, "Thy Kingdom come, thy will be done in earth as it is in Heaven." You and I, as Ambassadors, are responsible for bringing Heaven in the earth.

The Kingdom Covenant is between God (Father, Son, Holy Ghost) and the

Church (Bride). The Bride of Christ Jesus is co-heir/joint heir with Jesus. (Romans 8:17)

We are seated in Christ Jesus in Heavenly places right now at the right hand of our Father. How can the Bride know what the Bridegroom wants without engaging? How can the Bride know the Bridegroom without engaging? How can two people walk together except they be agreed? (Amos 3:3) The Bridegroom knows His Bride.

Our Father can engage everyone in the earth at the same time. He is omnipresent.

Yet not everyone engages with our Father. Why? Not everyone knows Him.

Why? The Church has not engaged with the people in the earth (world). If the people do not receive you, that is up to them. Jesus said to dust off your feet and keep it moving. (Matthew 10:14)

Except the Lord build the house, they labor in vain that built it; except the Lord keep the city, the watchman waketh but in vain. (Psalm 127:1)

As the Body of Christ, the Bride of Christ, we are to bring God's Kingdom into the earth through us. There isn't anyone sick, homeless, in jail, hungry, thirsty, nor naked in God's Kingdom. For I was hungry, you gave Me something to eat; I was thirsty, and you gave Me something to drink; I was a stranger, and you invited Me in; I was naked, and you clothed Me; I was sick and you visited Me [with help and ministering care]; I was in prison and you came to Me [ignoring personal danger]. (Matthew 25:35-36 AMP)

If we can be one with Jesus, then we can be one with each other. The God in you comes together with the God in me. We cannot come together in our flesh. That reaps corruption. We must come together in Spirit. We are Spirit housed in mortal flesh, having a human experience. We are not equal with God. We can become one with God in Spirit and in Truth. God wants to partner with us in bringing His Kingdom into the earth where it once was; the garden of Eden.

God is a God of love, order, justice, peace, joy, charity, patience, forgiveness, faithfulness, mercy, favor, and wrath.

When we say we are Christian, we are saying we are Christ-like.

We have benefits of being the sons of God and will have greater benefits when our Bridegroom removes us from the earth, so that He may destroy our enemies once and for all. There will be peace on earth. We can have peace now. I am talking about an internal peace.

Kingdom Covenant, marriage is about dominion in the earth; it's about being fruitful, multiplying, and filling the earth; it's about subduing the earth; (subdue means to bring under control). Satan wants to be in control. Satan wants to be worshipped. If he cannot, he will try to steal, kill, and destroy as long as you are following God.

This is about restoring Man to his rightful place. This is about preparing to reign with Jesus. This is what all the fuss is about, to put it plainly. We have already won and we must fight to keep it.

Adam, do you know who you are?

God calls each of us out of the darkness and into His glorious light. He has chosen each of us for a purpose. He has graced us to become His child. He has equipped us to be who we are called, chosen, and graced to become. We are called to be in the Body of Christ. We are called to be the Bride of Christ.

Kingdom Covenant is heavenly things.

Satan knows our power better than we do. Satan knows us better than we do. The garden of Eden was God's Kingdom in the earth. Satan recognized that. Keep in mind, Satan lived in Heaven. He was a part of God's Kingdom. The garden of Eden was another chance for him to rule and reign on God's throne.

We are a threat to Satan. Heaven is on our side. He knows that if we all knew who Jesus is, his time would be up. He knows as long as we are divided, he gets to wreak havoc a little longer. We should be angry about that, as children of God.

It has always been about Satan wanting to be worshipped, wanting to rule and reign; wanting to be like the Most High God. If Man knew who Man is, Satan would be in trouble.

Resist the devil and he shall flee. (James 4:7) Pride comes before destruction and a haughty spirit (arrogance) before a fall. (Proverbs 16:18)

Satan was thrown out of heaven. Jesus took dominion back from Satan. (Luke 10:18)

The third time will be total destruction. (Revelations 12:7-9; Daniel 7)

Satan does not like you and he's afraid of you. He's afraid that if you ever truly found out, came into the knowledge of who you are and whose you are, his time will be even more limited. When people do evil to other people, they are worshipping Satan. He is feeding off your evil.

2 Timothy 2:16 (AMP) But avoid all irreverent babble, and godless chatter [with its profane, empty words], for it will lead to further ungodliness; 17 and their teachings will spread like gangrene. So it is with Hymenaus and Philetus; 18 who have deviated from the truth. They claim that the resurrection has already taken place, and they undermine the faith of some. 19 Nevertheless, the firm foundation of God [which He has laid] stands [sure and unshaken despite attacks]; bearing this seal: "The Lord knows who are His; and "Let everyone who names the name of the Lord stand apart from wickedness and withdraw from wrongdoing."

Thus, those who are sanctified and ordained by God, while we were yet in our mothers' womb, to lead, teach, feed, mature, guide the household of faith, and to reach the lost; those who walk in darkness. We should be wholly reliant on the person of the Holy Ghost; God's Holy Spirit. Amen. The Holy Ghost knows the heart of God; therefore, He is the one we should be asking about the scriptures, the Word of God. It's okay to glean, to eat, to reason together with those God chose to lead. Coming together gives us a more complete picture of God (what God is saying in that season). It's not my opinion versus yours. It's what God revealed to you and to me. This is not a competition. The only person you should be in competition with is the person you were yesterday to be a better version of you today and a better version of you tomorrow.

Jesus instructed us to ask for daily bread. Just as the Israelites received manna from Heaven daily. Today is a present to be opened today; for tomorrow will take care of itself. God is already there, so there's no need to worry about tomorrow; no need to worry at all. (I am preaching to myself too) Each day is a gift. God's mercies are new every morning. Thank God.

The Bridegroom, Jesus Christ, looked beyond the cross, and saw me and you in sin, in trouble of our own making, diseased, stricken, impoverished and went to the cross. It was love for you and me that He pushed past being despised, hated, slapped, spit on, beat to the point where His own bones looked at him; a crown of thorns pressed down on His head, shamed, His beard snatched out of His face.

It was His sacrificial, unconditional, intentional, on purpose, purposeful love for you and me. The Bread of Heaven born in Bethlehem (House of Bread); the Chief Shepherd born in a manger. The Living Water sitting on top of a well waiting for a lost soul to quench her thirsting soul. Jesus. How could His Bride not love Him? The first Adam said, "God, it's that woman you gave me." Jesus, the last Adam, said, "I'll take her. I'll die for her." When the Roman soldier pierced Jesus' side with that spear, out came blood and water. Water to purify and the blood to redeem. Jesus with His arms stretched wide on the cross for His Bride. That's the Bridegroom. Jesus.

But He was wounded because of our sins, crushed because of our iniquities. He bore the chastisement that made us whole, and by His stripes we were healed. (Isaiah 53:5 Tanakh)

Love is faithful. Love is action. Faith without works is dead. Without Faith, it is impossible to please God. (James 2:14-26, Hebrews 11:6). Faith requires belief.

Abraham believed God and it was counted to him for righteousness. (Genesis 15:6 Hebrews 11:1, 6). Faith requires action. We sit down on chairs, couches, board planes, trains, automobiles and do not have a relationship with the builders. Do we think about or check before sitting down, or driving, or flying?

God created Man; yet do we believe, have faith, hope, trust?

Marriage, Covenant, is where we should have the most belief, faith, hope, trust in God. He is the author and finisher of our faith.

For in Him we live, and move, and have our being; as certain also of your own poets have said, For we are also His offspring. (Acts 17:28)

Covenant is an agreement. When you come into agreement with a person or multiple people, a contract or agreement is put in writing for all to sign.

KINGDOM COVENANT | Jill A. Woolford

As believers, we have the Bible, the word of God.

A few years back, someone sent me a story about a wealthy man who passed away. He was known for his priceless art collection. He had one son who died at a young age. This man adored his son. He had a butler, a manservant, if you will, who was loyal to this wealthy man and adored his son. So, there wasn't an heir to leave his wealth to, so the priceless art collection went to the auction house per the Will and Testament of the wealthy man. The manservant was present. The auction started out with a painting of the son. No one would bid. They insisted on seeing the priceless artwork they had their hearts set on. The manservant saw that no one was bidding on the son's portrait, so he decided to bid and the portrait went to him. The auctioneer's gavel went down and closed the auction. The people revolted and insisted on the auctioneer to bring out the priceless artwork. The auctioneer said the instructions were to auction the portrait of the son; and the one who purchases it gets the whole collection. So, the manservant, who was faithful, who loved the son got *everything.*

With the Son, you and I get *everything*.

Although we make mistakes, trip, stumble, and fall into sin, with the Son we get **everything**. "It Is Finished."

The Church is Eve – Mother of all living.

Our highest calling as the Church is to be the Bride of Christ. His rib, bone of His bones, flesh of His flesh, to become one with Jesus. To be presented to Him a glorious Church without spot, wrinkle, or blemish.

We are to be a battle ax to the kingdom of darkness, Satan's kingdom, this world we are in but not of; A mother gives birth, nurtures, protects, corrects, and chastens when necessary. Don't mess with her cubs.

A wife comes along the side of her husband, his rib, and they rule and reign together. A wife is to be submitted to her husband. The Bride is to be submitted to the Bridegroom. When Jesus submitted to His Father, our Father, He was given all power, and rose with the keys to death and hell. At His name, every knee shall bow in earth, under the earth, and in heaven. Our Father put all things under His feet. As His Bride, in the name of Jesus, we can ask anything of the Father and He will give it to us. We are Christians, Christ like. Jesus said, "When you see Me, you see the Father." When people see us, the Church, they should see Jesus. We are His lioness. He's the Lion of the Tribe of Judah.

Eve, do you know who you are? Let's go deeper. Adam, who told you that you were naked? Who have you been talking to? Do you know who you are? Why does Satan know your authority better than you do? That's why he tricked our Mother (Eve) into eating that fruit, then giving it to our Father (Adam). He stole the dominion, the authority God gave us. No worries. Jesus took it back and the Church has authority to take dominion in His name.

Where two are touching and agreeing on a thing, whatever you bind in the earth shall be bound in heaven; whatever you loose in the earth shall be loosed in heaven.

Church, what are you binding and loosing?

Where two or three are gathered in My name, there I shall be in the midst.

Jesus! There's power in that name. At the name of Jesus, every demon *must* flee.

In the name of Jesus, you are loosed to take dominion, take territory back from the kingdom of darkness. Snatch those souls from the pit of hell. Get your garden of Eden back. My Lord! No poverty, no diseases, no sickness, no illness, no violence, no lack, nothing missing. Shalom.

Do it now. Now, Church! Now! My God! My God!

The earth is the Lord's and the fullness thereof and they that dwell therein; yet the Lord God gave us dominion over the works of His hands. He told us to be fruitful, multiply, and fill the earth. Bring it into order, Adam. Do you know the authority you have as the Bride of Christ?

When God brings Kingdom husbands and Kingdom wives together, it's to take dominion, take territory; rule and rein together.

Do you know who you are, Adam? You are loosed in the name of Jesus to take dominion, take territory.

We are the Mother, so it's time to snatch those souls out of the pit of hell Satan has them trapped in, sold to sin. But God! It's time. Let's go! We got work to do. The harvest is ripe. Where are the reapers, the laborers? The benefits are greater than any job you can think of that's in the earth or will ever be. Protection. Provision. Chief Physician.

It's time, Church!

Chapter 1 | God Created Marriage

FOR PASTORS

The Pastor is the husbandman of the Church he/she is pastoring.

It is a marriage. It is the image of Jesus, the Bridegroom and the Church, His Bride.

Jesus intercedes for us daily. The weight on the Pastor is great.

Just as Aaron went into the Tabernacle before the Lord God for Israel, wearing the names of each tribe on his shoulders, chest, and heart. Aaron had two stones on each shoulder engraved with the names of each tribe (6 on one, 6 on the other), Jacob's 12 sons, 12 individual stones on his breastplate, over his heart with Urim and Thummim. On the mitre of gold, words that say, HOLINESS TO THE LORD. Aaron was consecrated for service to the Lord God. After Aaron was dressed, anointing oil was poured upon his head. Psalm 133:2, It is like the precious ointment upon the head, that ran down the beard, even Aaron's beard; that went down the skirts of his garment. That's why the woman with an issue of blood for 12 years said to herself, "If I could just touch the hem of His garment, I shall be made whole." (Matthew 9:20-21)

The Priest goes before the Lord with the weight of a nation on his shoulders, chest, and heart.

The weight of God's glory is heavy. Just as Moses needed Aaron and Hur to hold up his arms as Israel battled, so does the Priest when he's weary and not so weary.

When someone undermines the Pastor, husbandman, trying to win the hearts of the people, that person is committing adultery. Those that follow that person are committing adultery. Thus, you are committing adultery against God.

My sheep hear my voice; another they will not follow.

The Pastor is the husbandman. The First Lady is to assist or help; the help meet. They are to co-reign over the Ministry, as Adam and Eve were to co-reign, as Jesus and the Church to co-reign, are joint heirs.

God said, I will give you a Pastor according to My own heart. (Jeremiah 3:15) God searches the heart of man. (1 Chronicles 28:9; Romans 8:27; 1 Corinthians 2:10; Revelations 2:23) Woe unto the Pastors who scatter the sheep of My pasture. (Jeremiah 23:1-3)

To be married to a Pastor is another level of Grace. You have to be able to war in the Spirit. This isn't about, "Look at me," "I'm famous," "I'm a First Lady," "Bow down to me," "Serve me." No, no. Jesus said, let the greatest among you serve. You have to be able to speak into him as a man, as a Pastor, as a father. The spiritual warfare is on another level. Witches, warlocks, sorcerers, soothsayers will attack. Your prayer, intercession has to be on that level. You need to be able to discern the spirits. There's no taking a break from warfare. You have to be able to tell those demons, you cannot have my husband, my wife, my children, grandchildren. Yes, this means war. I'll go to hell and snatch them out. You have to have an, "I wish you would, I dare you, you don't know who you're messing with, I'm not the one, leap over here if you want" spiritual warfare.

Pastors, the ministry does **NOT** come before your spouse and children. Only God comes before your spouse and children. God must be sought to ask for wisdom to minister to your spouse and children. Do **NOT** make your spouse and children the mistress. When you are putting the ministry before your spouse, you are committing adultery. Adultery isn't just a physical act of intimacy; it is emotional abandonment as well. When God called Israel an adulteress nation; it wasn't because they stopped being physically intimate with God. They abandoned or turned their hearts from God to those false gods of the surrounding nations. They even sacrificed their children to those false gods and built altars. Your spouse and children are your *first* ministry. It has been a tradition that has been passed down that the ministry comes before spouse and children. That's why divorce amongst the Church is even greater than the world. First, did God **TRULY** say to marry the one you chose. If you're truly listening to God, thereby submitted, you will surely know that person has been specifically chosen, called and graced by God to be your spouse. That alone is a calling. Fast and pray and crucify your flesh. God knows what catches your eye, so to speak, and so does Satan.

Purpose

Why did God create Marriage?

Chapter 2

Chapter 2 | Purpose

The sole purpose is to rule and reign, bring order, Kingdom order into the earth.

God told us from the Beginning to *Be fruitful, Multiply, Fill the earth, Subdue it (bring into order) and Take dominion (rule).* These commands have been relegated to having children only; however, each of us were given both natural and spiritual gifts to be fruitful, multiply and fill the earth with.

1 Corinthians 12:1,4-11 (AMP) 1 Now about the spiritual gifts [the special endowments given by the Holy Spirit], brothers and sisters, I do not want you to be uninformed; 4 Now there are [distinctive] varieties of spiritual gifts [special abilities given by the grace and extraordinary power of the Holy Spirit operating in believers], but it is the same Spirit [who grants them and empowers believers] 5 And there are [distinctive] varieties of ministries and service, but it is the same Lord [who is served]. 6 And there are [distinctive] ways of working [to accomplish things], but it is the same God who produces all things in all believers [inspiring, energizing, and empowering them]. 7 But to each one is given the manifestation of the Spirit [the spiritual illumination and the enabling of the Holy Spirit] for the common good. 8 To one is given through the [Holy] Spirit [the power to speak] the message of wisdom, and to another [the power to express] the word of knowledge and understanding according to the same Spirit. 9 to another [wonder-working] faith [is given] by the same [Holy] Spirit, and to another the [extraordinary] gifts of healings by the one Spirit; 10 and to another the working of miracles, and to another prophecy [foretelling the future, speaking a new message from God to the people], and to another discernment of spirits [the ability to distinguish sound, godly doctrine from the deceptive doctrine of man-made religions and cults], to another various kinds of {unknown} tongues, and to another interpretation of tongues. 11 All these things [the gifts, the achievements, the abilities, the empowering] are brought about by one and the same [Holy] Spirit, distributing to each one individually just as He chooses.

Ephesians 4:4-11 (AMP) 4 There is one body [of believers] and one Spirit—just as you were called to one hope when called [to salvation] 5 one Lord, one faith, one baptism 6 one God and Father of us all who is [sovereign] overall and [working] through all and [living] in all 7 Yet grace [God's undeserved favor] was given to each one of us [not discriminately, but in different ways] in proportion to the measure of Christ's [rich and abundant] gift 8 Therefore it says, When He ascended on high, He led captivity captive, and He bestowed gifts on men; 9 (Now this expression, "He ascended," what does it mean except that He also had previously descended [from the heights of heaven] into the lower parts of the earth? 10 He who descended is the very same as He who also has ascended high above all the heavens, that He [His presence] might fill all things [that is, the whole universe]. 11 And [His gifts to the church were varied and] He Himself appointed some as apostles [special messengers, representatives], some as prophets [who speak a new message from God to the people], some as evangelists [who spread the good news of salvation], and some as pastors and teachers [to shepherd and guide and instruct], 12 [and He did this] to fully equip and perfect the saints (God's people) for works of service, to build up the body of Christ [the Church]

Adam and Eve were created to reign together in the earth. Adam and Eve were a foreshadowing of the Bridegroom, Jesus and His Bride, the Church. From the beginning, we were created to have dominion, to rule in the earth.

Reigning is about order, justice, peace, love, joy, charity, prosperity. Our main purpose here on earth is to bring God's Kingdom into the earth. There's order in Heaven. God's Kingdom is order; Seraphim, Cherubim, Gabriel, Michael, Warring and Messenger Angels; everyone knows what they are supposed to do and does it. For the Angels who rebelled, judgment was swift. (Ezekial 28 and Isaiah 14) The Apostle Peter stated there are Angels chained in darkness. (2 Peter 2:4; Jude 1:6) Jesus said he saw the devil, formally known as Lucifer, fall like lightning to the earth. (Luke 10:18) He was prideful. He wanted to exalt himself to God's throne. Lucifer said in his heart that he would ascend to the Most High God's throne and be like the Most High God. Lucifer wanted to be worshipped. He still does. He tricked Adam in the garden of Eden because he wanted to reign, which was God's kingdom in the earth.

As God's Kingdom Citizens, we are to bring God's Kingdom into the earth.

How? Kingdom principles (Matthew 25:35-40)

    Feed the hungry – anyone hungry in Heaven?

    Give water to the thirsty – anyone thirsty in Heaven?

    Clothe the naked – anyone naked Heaven?

Take in the stranger – anyone homeless in Heaven?

Take care of the widow and orphan – there's no such thing in Heaven.

Visit those in prison and in the hospital – there's no such thing in Heaven.

What we do in the earth is all preparation to reign with the King of Kings, the Lord of Lords. This is OJT – on-the-job training. We are destined to reign alongside the Bridegroom. We are supposed to be bone of his bones, flesh of his flesh. His rib. His Bride.

We are to occupy until Jesus returns. (Luke 19:11-13) Jesus told us to preach the Gospel in Jerusalem, Judea, Samaria, and the uttermost parts of the world. (Acts 1:8)

Jesus said, greater things will you do. What did Jesus do? Heal, deliver, set free, to name just a few. We are made in the image and after the likeness of God. We are to do what Jesus did. Jesus was God, yet He was man, so he walked and used boats to cross the sea of Galilee. We now have cars, trains, buses, airplanes, the internet, Wi-Fi, and social media.

If we're not doing it in the earth now, reigning that is, understanding and operating in our purpose, then, how are we to reign with Jesus when it's time?

Understanding and operating in Kingdom Covenant is very important.

We must understand our role here right now in the earth.

Man's idea of marriage is worldly and not Kingdom, and that's the problem. People don't know the true purpose of marriage. They think it's about pleasing each other. It's about subduing, bringing order, God's order into the earth.

Jesus didn't suffer extremely for each of us to waste our lives.

When the soldier pierced Jesus' side, out came water and blood, the water to purify and the blood to redeem us. Just as God put the man Adam to sleep to remove a rib to create woman, then present this creature to the man, who then declares, "Bone of my bones, flesh of my flesh; you shall be called woman because you came out of man." Therefore, shall a wife cause a man to leave his father and mother and cleave to his wife; and the two shall become one.

The highest, most important calling as children of God is to become the Bride of Christ; to learn to reign with our Bridegroom, Jesus.

Husbands

Who is he? What is his purpose?

Chapter 3

Chapter 3 | Husbands

Lead her like Abraham

Fight for her like Jacob

Care for her like Boaz

Love her like Christ

       J
       E
       S
       U
       S

H U S B A N D AND W I F E

       C
       H
       I
       L
       D
       R
       E
       N

Adam, do you know who you are? Take your rightful place, says the Lord!

Genesis
> 1:26 God said, Let us make man in our image, after our likeness: and let them have dominion over the fish of the sea, and over the fowl of the air, over the cattle, and over all the earth, and over every creeping thing that creepeth upon the earth

1:27 So God created man in His own image, in the image of God created He him; male and female created He them

1:28 And God blessed them, and God said unto them, Be fruitful, and multiply, and replenish the earth, and subdue it; and have dominion over the fish of the sea, and over the follow of the air, and over every living thing that moveth upon the earth

1:29 And God said, Behold, I have given you every herb bearing seed, which is upon the face of all the earth, and every tree, in which is the fruit of a tree yielding seed; to you it shall be for meat

2:7 And the Lord God formed man of the dust of the ground, and breathed into his nostrils the breath of life; and man became a living soul

2:8 And the Lord God planted a garden eastward of Eden; and there he put the man whom he had formed

2:15 And the Lord God took the man, and put him into the garden of Eden to dress it and to keep it

2:16 And the Lord God commanded the man, saying, Of every tree of the garden thou mayest freely eat

2:17 But of the tree of the knowledge of good and evil, thou shalt not eat of it: for in the day that thou eatest thereof thou shalt sure die

2:18 And the Lord God said, it is not good that the man should be alone; I will make him an help meet for him

2:19 And out of the ground the Lord God formed every beast of the field, and every fowl of the air; and brought them unto Adam to see what he would call them; and whatsoever Adam called every living creature, that was the name thereof

2:20 And Adam gave names to all cattle, and to the fowl of the air; and to every beast of the field; but for Adam there was not found an help meet for him.

2:21 the Lord God caused a deep sleep to fall upon Adam, and he slept;

and He took one of his ribs, and closed up the flesh; the rib, which the Lord God had taken from Man, made He a woman, and brought her unto the Man

2:22 And the rib, which The Lord God had taken from man, made he a woman, and brought her unto the man

2:23 Adam said this is now bone of my bones, and flesh of my flesh; she shall be called Woman because she came out of man

2:24 Therefore shall a man leave his father and mother, and shall cleave unto his wife: and they shall be one flesh

2:25 And they were both naked; the man and his wife; and were not ashamed.

Man was created in the image and after the likeness of God. We were made a little lower than the Angels.

When God brought the woman to the man, the man declared bone of my bones, flesh of my flesh, you shall be called Woman because you came out of Man; the man recognized his rib, his flesh.

Will you recognize your rib when God presents her to you? Will your spirit declare, "Bone of my bones, flesh of my flesh?" How does a man find or recognize his wife? It's spiritual. You will see in your wife what you need.

The Lord God could not find a help meet for Adam amongst His creation, so God created a help meet for him.

God knows exactly what and who His sons need, desire.

God knows the end from the beginning.

God knows the heart of Man.

God is the ultimate matchmaker. He just needs your "yes."

Just as God created, formed a wife for the first man (Adam), why wouldn't He create a wife for His sons today and present her to you?

The husband and wife in the garden were representative of Christ Jesus and the

Church, His Bride; a foreshadowing of what was to come.

Just as the husband and wife, male and female, are representative of Christ Jesus and the Church.

God said to Man (male & female) be fruitful, multiply and fill the earth. Subdue it (bring it into order). Take dominion (rule) over the fowls of the air, fish of the sea, and all that move, creeps upon the earth.

Man's purpose was and is to take care of God's creation.

The male was working, but why? Then, God gave him a wife (favor); now he had a purpose (a why) for what he was doing.

When God said, it's not good for Man to be alone, it was because he didn't have a purpose (a why) for what he was doing.

When Jesus said pray, Our Father which art in Heaven, Hallowed (Holy) be thy name; thy Kingdom come, thy will be done in earth as it is in Heaven. The only way to see God's Kingdom in the earth is that it has to be done in each of us, so God's Kingdom can come through us into the earth.

The garden of Eden was just that. . .until Satan.

Kingdom Covenant expressed by a marriage: the responsibility of the wife and the responsibility of the husband.

Ephesians 5:22-33

    22 Wives, submit yourselves unto your own husbands, as unto the Lord

    23 For the husband is the head of the wife, even as Christ is the head of the church: and he is the savior of the body

    24 Therefore as the church is subject unto Christ, so let the wives be to their own husbands in everything.

    25 Husbands, love your wives, even as Christ also loved the church, and gave himself for it.

    26 That he might sanctify and cleanse it with the washing of water by the word,

27 That he might present it to himself a glorious church, not having spot, or wrinkle, or any such thing; but that it should be holy and without blemish.

28 So ought men to love their wives as their own bodies. He that loveth his wife loveth himself.

29 For no man ever yet hated his own flesh; but nourisheth and cherisheth it, even as the Lord the church:

30 For we are members of his body, of his flesh, and of his bones.

31 For this cause shall a man leave his father and mother, and shall be joined unto his wife, and they two shall be one flesh.

32 This is a great mystery: but I speak concerning Christ and the church.

33 Nevertheless let every one of you in particular so love his wife even as himself; and the wife sees that she reverence her husband.

If you haven't noticed, the majority of the instructions, commandments, if you will, is to the Bridegroom, the husband. Why? Because Jesus paid it all at the cross. All the wife has to do is submit her will and respect her husband. Sounds simple, easy; yet if the husband loves and leads like Jesus, the wife should not have any issues with submission.

The husband is the priest of the home. The wife is his ezer, help meet. The husband is like Jesus, who is the head of the Church. The wife is like the Church, the Body of Christ. The children, grandchildren, etc. are the disciples.

The wife is submitted to her husband as the Church is submitted to Jesus. Jesus is submitted to the Father. Submission is powerful. Our Father gave Jesus authority and power over and in the earth, and under the earth. Submission has been abused, misunderstood. Submission is not subservient as man chooses to believe; to put woman under his foot. Man will not receive favor from God.

God does not demand us to do anything. We have free will. His love commands us to do His will.

Keep in mind, when you are speaking to your wife, you are talking to God's daughter.

A husband's love for his wife commands her to submit, not demand.

Jesus' *will* was and is submitted to the Father.

The husband's *will* is to be submitted to Jesus, just as Jesus is submitted to the Father. If the husband's *will* is not submitted to Jesus what will the wife be submitting to? The husband's flesh? With that scenario, God's Kingdom cannot be done in earth. The prince/ruler of darkness runs that marriage; hence the house.

The first man Adam blamed God for the Woman. The last man Adam, Jesus, went to the cross. They hung Him high, stretched Him wide; He hung His head, then He died; then the soldier pierced His side.

The first man Adam side was pierced to bring the Woman out of him.

The last man Adam's side was pierced to restore the Woman with the blood and water that poured out of His side. The Woman, the help meet, divine help, was created to reign with the Man. God opened up the side of the Man and removed his rib.

Love is commanding, not demanding. If you are demanding things to be done your way, that is <u>not</u> love. God is not in that. Demanding is control, mostly by a manipulative form of control. If you don't do this, I will not do that. I'm not going to talk to you, do for you, if you don't do this or that for me.

When God presents your wife to you, your spirit should be declaring, "Bone of my bones, flesh of my flesh."

God prepares the husband to receive his wife.

God gave our Father (Adam) purpose, responsibility before creating our Mother (Eve) for him. Then he had a reason for his purpose.

God gave our Father provision - a place to live and food to eat - before giving him his wife.

God arranges marriages just as Father God has chosen a Bride for His Son, Jesus.

She will be presented to Him at the marriage supper dressed in linen without spot or blemish - a glorious Bride. She will rule and reign with her Bridegroom.

Just like the first Adam was pierced in his side for his wife as was Jesus pierced in His side for His Bride.

Husband, your wife is your God-given favor, not your slave. She is your rib, not your backbone or foot bone.

Verses 25-26 The husband is to be like the Bridegroom: Sacrificial, sanctifying, cleansing with the washing of water by the Word of God; nourishing, cherishing.

Husband, speak the Word of God into your wife, over your wife.

The husband is to sanctify and cleanse his wife with the washing of water by the word.

Why marriages fail is that God is not invited to be a part of the Covenant. *Don't allow Satan to use you to bind your wife. You bind divine favor when you do that. God resists the proud and arrogant. How do you think God feels about how you treat His daughter?*

Proverbs 18:22 (AMP) He who finds a [true and faithful] wife finds a good thing and obtains favor and approval from the Lord

Proverbs 5:15-23 (AMP)
> 15 Drink water from your own cistern [of a pure marriage relationship] and fresh running water from your own well
>
> 16 Should your springs (children) be dispersed, as streams of water in the streets?
>
> 17 [Confine yourself to your own wife.] Let your children be yours alone, and not the children of strangers with you.
>
> 18 Let your fountain (wife) be blessed [with the rewards of fidelity], and rejoice in the wife of your youth,
>
> 19 And let her be as the loving hind and a graceful doe; let her breasts refresh and satisfy you at all times; always be exhilarated and delight in her love.
>
> 20 Why should you, my son, be exhilarated with an immoral woman, and embrace the bosom of an outsider (pagan)?

21 For the ways of man are directly before the eyes of the Lord, and He carefully watches all of his paths [all of his comings and goings]

22 The iniquities done by a wicked man will trap him; and he will be held with the cords of his sin

23 He shall die for lack of instruction (discipline); and in the greatness of his foolishness, he shall go astray and be lost

In other words, stay true to your wife…God knows all. God sees all.

Ecclesiastes 9:9 (Tanakh)

Enjoy happiness with a woman you love all the fleeting days of life that have been granted to you under the sun—all your fleeting days. For that alone is what you can get out of life and out of the means you acquire under the sun.

Psalm 128:3 (Tanakh)

Your wife shall be like a fruitful vine within your house; your sons, like olive saplings around your table

KJV Thy wife shall be as a fruitful vine by the sides of thine house: thy children like olive plants round about thy table

> *Pastor Jentzen Franklin: a woman is a multiplier. When a man gives a woman his seed, she will multiply it and give him a baby. Give a woman a house and she will multiply it and make it a home. Give a woman trouble and she will multiply it, pressed down, shaken together and running over, will she give it back to you. (LOL))*

An example that God chooses the wife.

This was a Christophany. Isaac was a foreshadowing of Jesus, the promised seed.

Genesis 24 Isaac's Bride *Abraham tasks his most faithful servant Eliezer to go to his hometown to find a wife for Isaac.*

When Abraham's wife Sarah died, and Isaac was 40 y.o., Abraham called his most trusted servant to find a wife for Issac. (Genesis 24). He had him swear not to look upon any of the Ites; Hittite, Jebuzite, etc., So, Abraham's most trusted servant stops at a well, and begins to pray to the God of his master, and was specific as to the type of woman. Yet God already had Isaac's wife picked out. He asked for a woman with a serving heart, essentially. As he was praying, a woman walks to the well to draw water and goes above and beyond what he requested. He then gave her gifts and asked for her father. Afterwards, they gathered to had a meal together. Abraham's most trusted servant told him why he was there and who sent him.

Abraham's most trusted servant's name was Eliezer; Rebekah was the woman who came to the well and did as Eliezer prayed for and more; Bethuel is the name of Rebekah's father. Eliezer means God's divine help or God is my help. Rebekah means to tie to, captivating beauty. Bethuel means house of God. So, Abraham sent God's divine help to the house of God to find a wife for Isaac.

A wife will cause a man to leave his father and mother and adjoin to his wife.

Just as God presented a wife to Adam, God did the same thing for Abraham's promised seed; just as God is doing right now for His Son, Jesus.

Matthew 19:3-6, 8, 9

> 19:3 The Pharisees also came unto Him, tempting Him, and saying unto Him, Is it lawful for a man to put away his wife for every cause?
>
> 19:4 And He answered and said unto them, Have ye not read, that he which made them at the beginning made them male and female.
>
> 19:5 And said, For this cause shall a man leave father and mother, and shall cleave to his wife: and they twain shall be one flesh?
>
> 19:6 Wherefore they are no more twain, but one flesh. What therefore God hath joined together, let not man put asunder.
>
> 19:8 He saith unto him, Moses because of the hardness of your hearts suffered you to put away your wives: but from the beginning it was not so.
>
> 19:9 And I say unto you, Whosoever shall put away his wife, except it be for fornication, and shall marry another, committeth adultery: and whoso marrieth married her which is put away doth commit adultery.

1 Corinthians 7:2-5

    1b It is good for a man not to touch a woman

    2 Nevertheless, to avoid fornication, let every man have his own wife, and let every woman have her own husband

    3 Let the husband render unto the wife due benevolence; and likewise, also the wife unto the husband

    4 The wife hath not power of her own body, but the husband: and likewise, also the husband hath not power of his own body, but the wife

    5 Defraud ye not one the other, except it be with consent for a time, that ye may give yourselves to fasting and praying; and come together again, that Satan tempt you not for your incontinency.

If you are not seeking God, then you are truly not seeking your wife. Your wife is not to be placed before God. Man is not to be placed before God. Man did not create you, bless you, give you dominion. Man did not go to the cross and die for you.

Your wife is not God Almighty, is not omnipotent, is not omnipresent; cannot be everywhere at the same time all the time.

When we say God knows the end from the beginning, do we believe that for every area of our lives? Or only for certain areas? Work, Career, Illness, Finances, to name a few

Can you trust God to choose your wife? Who did God call and set you apart to marry? To come into Covenant with? Covenant is a calling.

We say we're waiting on God for a car or a new car. We say we're waiting on God for a house. We say we're waiting on God for a financial miracle.

I don't hear many men say, "I'm waiting on God for my wife."

Are you allowing God to prepare you for your wife?

What are you doing while you're waiting?

Do you know what the Word of God says about a husband?

Chapter 3 | Husbands

Do you know what it means to be a husband?

Amos 3:3 How can two walk together unless they agree?

How can God bring two people together less they agree?

Why do we wait until an engagement to learn who we are and our purpose as Kingdom Covenant partners, so to speak? Do you know what it means to be the Bridegroom? Do you know what Covenant means?

Hebrews 13:4 Marriage is honorable in all, and the bed undefiled: but whoremongers and adulterers God will judge

Why did Satan approach the woman? Are you prepared to cover your wife?

Satan thinks the woman is the weaker vessel. Satan beguiled the woman with the same tricks he uses today; lust of the eyes, lust of the flesh, and the pride of life. Husband, cover your wife. Do not let just anyone approach your wife and engage her in conversation, just as the serpent did to Adam's wife in the garden of Eden. Satan's whole agenda is to destroy marriages.

1 Peter 3:7 AMP (read vs 1-8)

In the same way, you husbands, live with your wives in an understanding way [with great gentleness and tact, and with an intelligent regard for the marriage relationship], as with someone physically weaker, since she is a woman. Show her honor and respect as a fellow heir of the grace of life, so that your prayers will not be hindered or ineffective.

2 Corinthians 6:14-15 Do not be unequally bound together with unbelievers [do not make mismatched alliances with them, inconsistent with your faith] . For what partnership can righteousness have with lawlessness? Or what fellowship can light have with darkness? 15 What harmony can there be between Christ and Balial (Satan)? Or what does a believer have in common with an unbeliever?

Unevenly yoked: there are times God will have a Believer joined to an Unbeliever...for His purpose. God knows that the Believer will pray for, speak into the Unbeliever. God has plans for that Unbeliever. So, God will bring a Believer and an Unbeliever together; and the Believer will represent the Love of God to the Unbeliever. The Believer will cause the Unbeliever to seek God because of the Love of God in the Believer and flowing through the Believer.

There are times where God will remove an Unbeliever from the Believer's life because that Unbeliever is a hindrance to the Believer's destiny, purpose God has for that Believer.

Even Believers can be unequally yoked.

There's a weight that is on the husband. There's a weight that is on the wife. There will be times when the husband will carry some of the weight of his wife. There will be times when the wife will carry some of the weight of her husband.

Marriage has a cross whereas the flesh must be crucified in order to live out and walk in the principles of Kingdom Covenant.

This isn't about who is supposed to cook, clean, take out the trash, get up in the middle of the night for a crying baby, or a child that got scared. Who washes dishes, or takes out the garbage are earthly things. Yes, we must take care of home; however, that's not the focus. Satan wants you focused on mundane things, arguing over mundane things so you wouldn't focus on him, what he's doing.

Covenant, Kingdom Covenant, is heavenly things.

This is about bringing God's Kingdom into the earth.

The garden of Eden was God's Kingdom in the earth. There was order, peace, and harmony, not lack; everything was provided beforehand.

God will not send the wife to the husband unless there is provision. The wife will then multiply the provision because she brings God's favor, divine favor with her. (Be fruitful, multiply, and fill the earth)

Kingdom Covenant is a calling.

You are called

You are chosen

You are graced

You are equipped…to be a specific woman's husband. She is your wife, no one else's, yours. You are her husband, no one else's, her husband.

Satan knows your power better than you do. Satan knows you better than you do.

Adam, do you know who you are?

The garden of Eden was God's Kingdom in the earth. Satan recognized that. Keep in mind, Satan lived in Heaven. He was a part of God's Kingdom. The garden of Eden was another chance for him to rule and reign on God's throne.

We are a threat to Satan. Heaven is on our side. This is a spiritual battle.

As Apostle Paul says, there is no good thing in the flesh. He crucified the flesh daily. (Romans 7:18-20 *For I know that in me (that is, my flesh) dwelleth no good thing: for to will is present with me; but how to perform that which is good I find not. 19 For the good that I would I do not; but the evil which I would not, that I do. 20 Now if I do that I would not, it is no more I that do it, but sin that dwelleth in me.)*

Matthew 16:24 *Then said Jesus unto His disciples, If any man will come after me, let him deny himself, and **take up his cross and follow me.***

Galatians 5:16-26 *This I say then, Walk in the Spirit, and ye shall not fulfill the lust of the flesh. 17 For the flesh lusteth against the Spirit, and the Spirit against the flesh; and these are contrary to the other: so that ye cannot do things that we would. 18 But if ye be led of the Spirit, ye are not under the law. 19 Now the works of the flesh are manifest, which are these; Adultery, fornication, uncleanness, lasciviousness, 20 idolatry, witchcraft, hatred, variance, emulations, wrath, strife, seditions, heresies, 21 envyings, murders, drunkenness, revelings, and such like of the which I tell you before, as I have also told you in time past, that they which do such things shall not inherit the Kingdom of God. 22 But the fruit of the Spirit is love, joy, peace, longsuffering, gentleness, goodness, faith, 23 meekness, temperance: against such there is no law. 24 And they that are Christ's have crucified the flesh with the affections and lusts. 25 If we live in the Spirit, let us also walk in the Spirit. 26 Let us not be desirous of vain glory, provoking one another, envying one another.*

Matthew 26:41 *Watch and pray, that ye enter not into temptation: the spirit indeed is willing, but the flesh is weak.*

Do not leave a chink in your armour for the devil to use. (Ephesians 6:10-18)

Guard your tongue. Ask the Holy Ghost to guard your tongue. (James 3)

Pray before you speak. It's okay to be angry, but sin not. Do not let the sun set on your wrath. (Ephesians 4:26) In other words, do not hold onto your anger and let it simmer and pour out on the next day. The enemy will give you some thoughts, some suggestions on how you should handle your feelings. Do not let a temporary situation cause you to make a permanent decision.

Just as God is preparing the Bride for the Bridegroom, God prepares his sons and daughters to be the Bridegrooms and the Brides. This is all preparation to reign with Christ Jesus. If you cannot reign together in the earth as husband and wife, how can you then reign with Christ Jesus?

When man and woman stand at the altar before God to come into Covenant, that man and that woman come as a husband and a wife.

When you choose what your flesh wants, you'll get hell.

Galatians 6:7-8 Be not deceived; God is not mocked: for whatsoever a man soweth, that shall he also reap; 8 For he that soweth to the flesh shall of the flesh reap corruption; but he that soweth to the Spirit shall of the Spirit reap life everlasting

When you allow God to choose, you are in the Spirit.

It is not about what your flesh wants. It's about the Kingdom of Heaven.

You cannot marry just anyone. If that person does not have the missing ingredients to your purpose, then what God has purposed for you will not be whole; your purpose will be delayed; there will be friction constantly; it will feel like the gates of hell is in your home.

The person you want to be with so bad may have the ingredients to make pizza, but you need the rest of the ingredients to make a cake. The person has the cheese and the dough, but you need sugar and vanilla extract and perhaps a pinch of salt; and a stick of butter. She needs the tomato sauce and seasoning, and you have flour, eggs, milk, a stick of butter, and a pinch of salt. You will not like the taste of that pizza when you put the ingredients you have together with the ingredients she has and surely not the taste of that cake.

God knows what you need and when you need it. The oven has to be preheated. You may even need the right oven first and the right pans and the mixer, metaphorically speaking.

God has given each person purpose. When God aligns people, places and things, it is to fulfill your God-given purpose. There are people that are gifted but are not walking in their purpose. You can see it by the fact that they think the world revolves around them. That is self-fulfilling, selfish. Your purpose, primarily, is to bring God's Kingdom into the earth. God is a God of order, purpose.

If you did not have a relationship with God, then how can you have a relationship with His daughter? Did God choose your wife?

If you do not invite God, then you invited all the hell you want.

Where two or three are gathered in His name, there He shall be in the midst.

Where two are touching and agreeing on a thing. (Matthew 18:19-20)

Before I formed thee in the belly, I knew thee; and before thou camest forth out of the womb I sanctified thee, and I ordained thee a prophet unto the nations. (Jeremiah 1:5-8) What did God set you apart, appointed, choose you to be.

> *"Don't expect anyone to be faithful to you if they aren't faithful to God."*
> *-Pastor John F. Hannah*

How is your prayer life? Do you have one? Do not assume because you see someone in God's house that they have a prayer life. Life will give you a prayer life; trials and tribulations. Do you pray together and for each other in the engagement process (stages)?

If you're constantly quitting on God, what else are you or would you quit when it gets tough? Love does not abandon ship. Love keeps the ship floating.

The storms will rock and toss the ship. If you call on Jesus, speak peace be still, Jesus will get you through the storms as a single person and as a couple. If you have a prayer life, Jesus is in the boat with you. The Holy Ghost that dwells in you and with you will guide you through or around the storms. If you do not have a prayer life, you will set the course of dysfunction for generations.

God is a God of generations. He doesn't just look at (consider) you and your wife. He looks at Abraham, Isaac, and Jacob.

A wise man leaves an inheritance for his children's children. (Proverbs 13:22;

Ecclesiastes 2:26; Job 27:16-17)

Knowing who and whose you are will absolutely change your life. You cannot have healthy relationships when you're not healthy; mind, heart, spirit and body.

3 John v2, Beloved, I wish above all things that thou mayest prosper and be in health, even as your soul prosper

(AMP) says, "good health [physically] just as I know your soul prospers [spiritually]

Romans 12:1 (AMP)…Present your bodies [dedicating all of yourselves, set apart] as a living sacrifice, holy and well-pleasing to God, which is your rational (logical, intelligent) act of worship

1 Corinthians 3:16 Know ye not, that ye are the temple of God, and that the Spirit of God dwelleth in you

1 Corinthians 6:13, 15-20…13b Now the body is not for fornication, but for the Lord; and the Lord for the body.
- 15 Know ye not that your bodies are the members of Christ? Shall I then take the members of Christ, and make them the members of an harlot? God forbid.

- 16 What? Know ye not that which is joined to an harlot is one body? For two, saith He, shall be one flesh.

- 17 But he that is joined unto the Lord is one spirit.

- 18 Flee fornication. Every sin that a man doeth is without the body, but he that committeth fornication sinneth against his own body

- 19 What? Know ye not that your body is the temple of the Holy Ghost which is in you, which ye have of God, and ye are not your own?

- 20 For ye are bought with a price; therefore glorify God in your body, and in your spirit, which are God's.

1 Corinthians 7:2-5

1 Now concerning the things whereof ye wrote unto me: It is good for a man not to touch a woman

2 Nevertheless, to avoid fornication, let every man have his own wife, and let every woman have her own husband.

3 Let the husband render unto the wife due benevolence; and likewise also the wife unto the husband

4 The wife hath not power of her own body, but the husband: and likewise also the husband hath not power of his own body, but the wife

5 Defraud ye not one the other, except it be with consent for a time, that ye may give yourselves to fasting and prayer; and come together again, that Satan tempt you not for your incontinency

Areas that break up marriages – Dr. Jamal-Harrison Bryant

1. *Income*
2. *Intimacy (frequency, quality, quantity, fidelity). The bedroom is undefiled*
3. *Imagination (undiscussed expectations)*

Matthew 19:4-6

v.6…what God brought together, let no man put asunder.

God gave men responsibility. Men are to lead, cover, protect, and provide. We are to go where God tells us, leads us. Do not leave your wife uncovered, unprotected, and without provision.

Lead her like Abraham to a land where God tells you to go. God blessed Abraham because of his obedience. Many nations came from Abraham, a man who was childless. His wife was barren in her womb, but God. God will allow some things to happen so He can show up and show He is God. God opened his wife's womb and she bore him a son. Abraham wasn't perfect. He made some mistakes. He tried to help God out, as we often do.

Fight for her like Jacob

Jacob worked 14 years for his wife, Rachel. This is why the bridegroom lifts the veil from the bride, so he can see for sure who he's marrying.

Care for her like Boaz

Boaz protected and provided for Ruth. He told the young men not to touch her. Boaz noticed Ruth while she was gleaning the fields. She was working to bring home food for her and her mother in law. Boaz heard of her reputation; how she left behind all she knew, her family and her home, a familiar place; a familiar people, familiar gods.

Love her like Christ

Jesus sacrificed His life for His Bride so that His Bride would be redeemed, made whole, have life abundantly, to prosper and be in good health as His Bride's soul prospers.

Healed. Delivered. Whole. Casting all your cares upon Him for He cares for you

When you come together, as a broken person, with someone who is also broken, that is twice the toxicity. You're actually in a relationship with the female version of you. You end up enabling each other, then no one gets made whole.

Are you truly born again? Have you truly given Jesus all your cares? Come to me all those that are heavy laden, I will give you rest. (Matthew 11:28-30)

Jeremiah 8:22 Is there no balm in Gilead; is there not a physician there? Why then is not the health of the daughter (Zion) of my people recovered?

1 Peter 5:7 casting all your cares upon Him; for He careth for you.

2 Corinthians 4:2 But have renounced the hidden things of dishonesty, not walking in craftiness, nor handling the Word of God deceitfully; but by manifestation of the truth commending ourselves to every man's conscience in the sight of God

What are you renouncing? Have you decided that you will start your marriage with a clean slate, so to speak? Have you ejected, rejected past hurts, pain, disappointments, or relationships gone wrong because they weren't supposed to be hurt, rejection, unforgiveness, bitterness, or uncleanness? What are you bringing with you that you should not?

Know the difference between flesh and Spirit. The flesh wars against the Spirit; the Spirit wars against the flesh. (Galatians 5:17; Matthew 26:4). What are you feeding? Your flesh? Your Spirit? (Galatians 6:8; 1 Peter 2:12)

Have you left your past in your past? God will **not** introduce you to your Kingdom wife until you allow Him to purge you from all uncleanness, ungodliness, and remove all those skeletons from your closet.

Repent. Pray. Seek deliverance (Renounce). Healing (Purging).

Speak the Word of God over and into your life.

Satan is here to steal, kill, and destroy by whatever means necessary. If he cannot kill you while in your mother's womb, he will find a way by attacking your identity – who you are, are you male or female; violence, perversion, slavery, divorce, idolatry, adultery, pride, arrogance, division, strife, anger, drugs, alcohol. If Satan controls your identity, he controls your life. Knowing who and whose you are is a must, not a maybe.

Keep in mind....

Marriage does not correct the mess you made with your loins. Fornication is not solved by marrying that person. The mess you made only gets amplified. Years down the road, you'd be trying to figure out what happened. You chose with your loins, your lust. Then, you're telling everybody God blessed you with this person. You realize after you said, "I do" that you really didn't hear from God. It was your flesh, your lusts. Now what? Do you continue to perpetuate the fraud? Or do you confess you were wrong as to who you listened to? Did God really say?

If the woman you asked to marry you gave you an ultimatum, "marry me or I'm leaving," "all of this will fall apart without me," that's not your wife. That's a witch. Manipulation is witchcraft. She's not of God or from God.

If you move forward, she becomes your god. Now, you're in idolatry and adultery. That woman has become your idol, hence idolatry. You put a woman before God, thus, you committed adultery.

God doesn't say, choose me or else. God says, choose me because I love you. I want you to have life and have it more abundantly. I want you to live with me forever. There will be no peace on earth. There will be no peace in that marriage. You will be in bondage.

God sees what attracts you. God knows what attracts you. And so does Satan because you tell him with your words and show him by your actions. God will prepare you then introduce you to who He chose for you. Satan will parade the imitation in your face until you give in.

God will put an open book test before you. You put the Word of God on that test. Satan will keep coming, sending imitations waiting for you to fail. It's not a multiple choice test. The answer is the Word. So, are you going to put the Word on the test? Or choose with your flesh? Yes, you still have a choice. You can align with God, or choose your flesh. Flesh is your sin nature. God is Spirit. Are you going to walk with God? Or go the way of the world, which is Satan?

Do not allow a temporary season of being single make you feel loneliness and just anybody is better than nobody. You'll find yourself 10, 15, 20, 25 years down the road trying to figure out what you were thinking, looking at each other upside the head. Then, you decide to stay because you don't want to start over or be alone. Some of you will choose to hold onto that person because you poured so much into that person. You don't want somebody else to benefit from it. Seriously?! Then, you try to make that person your indentured servant, slave, until they work off whatever that person owes you. Seriously?! I know it's true. I said once that I didn't want another woman benefitting from my hard work. I was building an organization and if he was cheating on me or things just didn't work out, that heifer wasn't going to be in my face smiling, benefitting from my hard work. Then, I grew up in Jesus.

You don't own anyone. You don't even own yourself. Learn from it. Grow up in Jesus from it. Life will give you lessons. You were bought with a price; the blood of Jesus.

Dating

Dating is you looking. God didn't tell us to go out looking. He who finds a wife finds a good thing and receives favor from the Lord. Adam didn't go looking for Eve. God created Eve for Adam. He found her when God presented her to him. We don't choose God. God calls us. Our Father chooses the Bride for the Bridegroom. God already knows who is for who because He knows what He put in each of us for His purpose. He knows our hearts. We get the benefits. When we're out looking, dating, do we truly know what or who we're looking for? We have lists, preferences, non-negotiables, and so forth. What does that have to do with the Kingdom of God? Do you know who you are? Do you know what's in you? Do you know your purpose? Do you think your job, career, work is your purpose? Are you passionate about what you do? Are you called to what you do? Do you know what's in you? How do you know what you're looking for? Will you know when you find her? Can you, or would you declare, "this is now bone of my bones, flesh of my flesh?" Keep in mind, the man declares that, not the woman. The husband should be looking at a mirror reflection of himself, his purpose.

If you don't know who you are, your purpose, then how do you know what you're looking for?

Where are you, Adam?

Is it your spirit man looking? Or are you being led by your flesh? Covenant is Kingdom. Those who worship God must worship Him in Spirit and in Truth, not flesh. Flesh must be crucified daily. Flesh is your sin nature. Marriage does not correct what your flesh chose, it amplifies it more.

You have all these flesh marriages out there that grieves your spirit man, that you tied your spirit man to and wonder why the next relationship didn't work out. You've been committing adultery over and over again. You're like a polygamist.

Consecrate Yourself

Consecration is purification; you don't do anything with anyone; it's preparation for Kingdom Covenant. If God revealed to you who He has chosen to be your wife, you then will allow God to prepare you for that person; even if God has not yet revealed your wife, and your desire is to be married, you must still be prepared, consecrated. You don't date. You don't flirt. You are called. You are chosen. You are graced for that specific person. God will teach you about, show you who she is, and the purpose for bringing the two of you together if you listen to and allow God to do what He does. It's not easy. I can testify to that. I ran out of patience a few times. Like, when? Then, God will show me something else I need to work on. I did not flirt. I did not date. I made sure I let the men who approached me know that I am not available. I am betrothed; God has already chosen my husband; that I am promised to someone already.

Have you divorced your previous wife(ves) in the Courts of Heaven? God is the Judge of Judges. He is the Just Judge. You may not have legally married that person, but you have sexual spiritual ties with her. Ask God to divorce you from that person(s). You are married by Biblical standards. You cannot take other people into your marriage, especially not a Kingdom Covenant. God will not allow it. There is no shame. There is no more condemnation in Christ Jesus. (Romans 8:1). Old things are passed away; behold all things are new. (2 Corinthians 5 14-21)

Make sure you are a whole, healed, delivered, born-again believer before coming together with someone; do not even date. Allow God to do a perfect work in you. You can be fine, handsome, dressed well, and be full of hell. Stop giving Satan credit and ammunition for what is going on inside of you. Seek the healer, Dr. Jesus. You must be made whole, then, you will be introduced to your wife who is whole.

When you were called out of the world, the world should have been left behind, so *DO NOT* take the concepts, systems of the world and try to blend it, marry it to the Word of God. Each of us should have divorced the world once we were called out. One cannot truly say I am born again, I am a new creature in Christ Jesus, yet try to blend, marry, if you will, the world to the Word of God. No. Be not conformed to the world, but be ye transformed by the renewing of your mind. We are supposed to be Christ-like, have the mind, heart, and ways of Jesus.

Otherwise, you are committing adultery against God. Yes, you can commit adultery against God. It's not just between husband and wife. "Thou shalt not commit adultery" is one of the commandments God gave in Exodus (20:14, cr Jeremiah 3:8). You're cheating on God with Satan. Adultery is a physical and emotional abandonment.

PRAYERS

Lord God, I renounce sin, trespasses, and iniquities in the name of Jesus.

Lord God, I renounce fornication, adultery, idolatry, masturbation, bitterness, anger, and hate in the name of Jesus.

Lord God, I renounce unforgiveness, envy, jealousy, pride, and arrogance in the name of Jesus.

Lord God, I renounce murder, division, strife, excessive alcohol, wine, spirits, and eating in the name of Jesus.

Lord God, I renounce smoking and drugs in the name of Jesus.

Lord God, as my heavenly Father, I ask that you break every vow I made knowingly and unknowingly that is contrary to Your Word and purpose for my life in the name of Jesus.

Lord God, I ask You to divorce me from my spiritual wife(ves) in the name of Jesus.

Lord God, I ask You to teach me what I should be eating and drinking so that I may prosper and be in good health as my soul prospers in the name of Jesus.

Lord God, I receive Your love for me, Your peace that passes all understanding, and Your joy that is unspeakable in the name of Jesus.

Lord God, I ask You to heal my soul and body, and renew in me a right spirit in Jesus name.

Lord God, I want to be whole that I may be of service to Your Kingdom in the name of Jesus.

Lord God, I ask You to baptize me with Your Holy Spirit in the name of Jesus; that I will walk in Your ways and speak Your ways in the name of Jesus, so I may hear Your heart in the name of Jesus.

All these things I pray in the name of Jesus Christ.

Amen. Amen. Amen.

Lord, I speak to those natural and spiritual gifts You put in your son while he was yet formed in his mother's womb. In the name of Jesus, arise, wake up gifts, be fruitful, multiply, and fill the earth. Not by might, not by power, by the Spirit of the Lord. Take your place in the earth. You shall thrive and live out your Kingdom purpose, in the name of Jesus Christ; It is so and so it is.

Amen. Amen. Amen.

Wife

Who is she? What is her purpose?

Chapter 4

Chapter 4 | Wife

Prepare like Esther

Honor like Ruth

Pray as bold as Hannah

Go to war like Deborah

Expect the impossible like Sarai

Sit at Jesus' feet like Mary

        J
        E
        S
        U
        S

H U S B A N D AND *W I F E*

        C
        H
        I
        L
        D
        R
        E
        N

Acts 17:28, For in Him we live, and move, and have our being; as certain also of your own poets have said, For we are also His offspring.

Eve, do you know who you are? Take your rightful place, says the Lord!

Genesis

1:26 God said, Let us make man in our image, after our likeness: and let them have dominion over the fish of the sea, and over the fowl of the air, over the cattle, and over all the earth, and over every creeping thing that creepeth upon the earth

1:27 So God created man in His own image, in the image of God created He him; male and female created He them

1:28 And God blessed them, and God said unto them, Be fruitful, and multiply, and replenish the earth, and subdue it; and have dominion over the fish of the sea, and over the follow of the air, and over every living thing that moveth upon the earth

1:29 And God said, Behold, I have given you every herb bearing seed, which is upon the face of all the earth, and every tree, in which is the fruit of a tree yielding seed; to you it shall be for meat

2:7 And the Lord God formed man of the dust of the ground, and breathed into his nostrils the breath of life; and man became a living soul

2:8 And the Lord God planted a garden eastward of Eden; and there he put the man whom he had formed

2:15 And the Lord God took the man, and put him into the garden of Eden to dress it and to keep it

2:16 And the Lord God commanded the man, saying, Of every tree of the garden thou mayest freely eat

2:17 But of the tree of the knowledge of good and evil, thou shalt not eat of it: for in the day that thou eatest thereof thou shalt sure die

2:18 And the Lord God said, it is not good that the man should be alone; I will make him an help meet for him

2:19 And out of the ground the Lord God formed every beast of the field, and every fowl of the air; and brought them unto Adam to see what he would call them; and whatsoever Adam called every living creature, that was the name thereof

Chapter 4 | Wife

2:20 And Adam gave names to all cattle, and to the fowl of the air; and to every beast of the field; but for Adam there was not found an help meet for him.

2:21 the Lord God caused a deep sleep to fall upon Adam, and he slept; and He took one of his ribs, and closed up the flesh; the rib, which the Lord God had taken from Man, made He a woman, and brought her unto the Man

2:22 And the rib, which The Lord God had taken from man, made he a woman, and brought her unto the man

2:23 Adam said this is now bone of my bones, and flesh of my flesh; she shall be called Woman because she came out of man

2:24 Therefore shall a man leave his father and mother, and shall cleave unto his wife: and they shall be one flesh

2:25 And they were both naked; the man and his wife; and were not ashamed.

When God brought the woman to the man, the man declared bone of my bones, flesh of my flesh, you shall be called Woman because you came out of Man; the man recognized his rib, his flesh. When God sends a man his wife, the man recognizes his rib, his flesh.

When Solomon wrote in Proverbs; He who finds [a and faithful] wife finds a good thing and obtains favor and approval from the Lord. (Proverbs 18:22)

When God planted the Garden of Eden in the earth, that was God's Kingdom in the earth. When Man sinned through disobedience, Man had to be removed. Sin cannot touch a Holy God. A Holy God cannot touch sin.

In the Beginning, God created Man – Adam – both male and female. Before God created Adam, He planted a garden. God gave provision before He created Man.

Why did Satan approach the woman?

The first man Adam blamed God for the woman. The last man Adam (Jesus) went to the cross to restore what was lost, stolen in the Garden. Kingship. Lordship. To restore the Woman, who is the Bride of Christ.

Satan is here to steal, kill, and destroy the seed of the Woman.

The first man Adam was pierced to bring the Woman out of him.

The last man Adam's side was pierced to restore the Woman with the blood and water that poured out of His side; water to purify and the blood to redeem. The Woman, the help meet, divine help, was created to reign with the Man.

The Word of God says that we are joint heirs with Christ Jesus. We, the Ekklesia (Church), was called out of the darkness into His glorious Light.

We fell into darkness because of our Father and Mother's disobedience.

Just as Satan used the serpent in the garden of Eden to beguile our Mother, he uses two-legged serpents, many that are close to you or close enough to you to steal, kill, and destroy.

It was the Woman who was deceived by Satan, who then caused her husband to disobey God. Jesus came to restore the Woman to her rightful place; and that is to reign with her husband. She cannot reign until she is restored.

Kingdom Covenant expressed by a marriage: the responsibility of the wife and the responsibility of the husband.

Ephesians 5:22-33

> 22 Wives, submit yourselves unto your own husbands, as unto the Lord
>
> 23 For the husband is the head of the wife, even as Christ is the head of the church: and he is the savior of the body
>
> 24 Therefore as the church is subject unto Christ, so let the wives be to their own husbands in everything.
>
> 25 Husbands, love your wives, even as Christ also loved the church, and gave himself for it.
>
> 26 That he might sanctify and cleanse it with the washing of water by the word,
>
> 27 That he might present it to himself a glorious church, not having spot, or wrinkle, or any such thing; but that it should be holy and without blemish.

28 So ought men to love their wives as their own bodies. He that loveth his wife loveth himself.

29 For no man ever yet hated his own flesh; but nourisheth and cherisheth it, even as the Lord the church:

30 For we are members of his body, of his flesh, and of his bones.

31 For this cause shall a man leave his father and mother, and shall be joined unto his wife, and they two shall be one flesh.

32 This is a great mystery: but I speak concerning Christ and the church.

33 Nevertheless let every one of you in particular so love his wife even as himself; and the wife see that she reverence her husband.

The husband and wife in the garden of Eden were representative of Christ Jesus and the Church. (His Bride); a foreshadowing of what was to come.

If you haven't noticed, the majority of the instructions, if you will, is to the Bridegroom.

The husband is the priest of the home. The wife is his ezer, help meet. The husband is like Jesus, who is the head of the Church. The husband is to sanctify and cleanse his wife with the washing of water by the word. The wife is like the Church, the Body of Christ. **The children, grandchildren, etc. are the disciples.**

The wife is submitted to her husband as the Church is submitted to Jesus. Jesus is submitted to the Father. Submission is powerful. Our Father gave Jesus authority, power, and dominion over and in the earth, and under the earth. Submission has been abused, misunderstood. Submission is not subservient as man chooses to believe; to put woman under his foot. ***A husband's love for his wife commands her to submit, not demand.***

Demanding is control, mostly by a manipulative form of control; i.e., If you don't do this, I will not do that. I'm not going to talk to you, do for you, if you don't do this or that for me.

When God brings man and woman together, the man's spirit should be declar-

ing, "Bone of my bones, flesh of my flesh."

Psalm 111:9 He sent redemption unto His people: He hath commanded His covenant forever; holy and reverend is His name. Reverend means to have a deep respect

Apostle Paul stated in verse 33 that the wife is to reverence her husband. Reverence means to be in "awe."

Christ Jesus, the Lamb of God, slain before the foundations of the world, went to the cross to redeem mankind. His side was pierced just like the first man Adam. The first man Adam blamed God for the woman. The last man Adam, as Jesus is called, died for His Bride; out came water and blood to purify and redeem His Bride.

Most of the instructions are given to the Bridegroom because it was God the Father, Son, and Holy Ghost that decided this was how Man was to be redeemed.

Jesus cried on that cross, "It is finished." What was finished? EVERYTHING.

When you are talking to your husband, you are talking to God's son. What you're doing to your husband, you're doing it to God's son; both good and evil. When man and woman come into Kingdom Covenant, God essentially becomes your Father-in-love. Love is God's law. God's laws are His commandments. God does not demand us to do anything. We have free will. God's love commands us to do His will.

Just as Satan beguiled the woman, Satan has been attacking the Church, the Bride of Christ, the woman. Satan thinks the woman is the weaker vessel. Satan beguiled the Woman with the same tricks he uses today; lust of the eyes, lust of the flesh, and the pride of life.

God said that man should not be alone; however there wasn't anyone suitable amongst all His creations, so God created a help meet for him. God knows exactly what and who His sons and daughters need, desire. God knows the end from the beginning. God knows the heart of Man. God is the ultimate matchmaker. He just needs your "yes."

Will you trust God to choose your husband?

Who did God call and set you apart to marry, to come into Covenant with?

If you are not seeking God, then you are not truly preparing for your husband.

You believe God for a car, a house, a job, finances, healing, but not for your husband? You believe God for worldly things but not for Kingdom things, Kingdom authority, Kingdom appointment.

Seek ye first the Kingdom of God and His righteousness; and all you need will be provided. Husband. Children. Work/Business/Ministry. Hobbies. Everything you do, do it unto God. Your husband is not to be placed before God. Man is not to be placed before God. Man did not create you, bless you, give you dominion. Man did not go to the cross and die for you.

Your husband is not God Almighty, is not omnipotent, is not omnipresent; cannot be everywhere at the same time all the time.

When we say God knows the end from the beginning, do we believe that for every area of our lives? Or only for certain areas? Work, Career, Illness, Finances.

Wherefore they are no more twain (two), but one flesh. What therefore God hath joined together, let no man put asunder (Matthew 19:3-6). What God hath joined together, not man. God brings husband and wife together, not man.

God knows the end from the beginning. (Isaiah 46:10)

God knows what we need before we ask. (Matthew 6:8)

We are to bring God's Kingdom into the earth. (Matthew 6:9-13)

Kingdom Covenant is God's will and purpose in the earth...through husband and wife. Just as husband and wife are to become one, so is the plan, purpose that the Bridegroom and His Bride, the Church, are to become one. How? Engagement.

God Arranges Marriages

When Abraham's wife Sarah died, and Isaac was 40 y.o., Abraham called his most trusted servant to find a wife for Issac. (Genesis 24). He had him swear not to look upon any of the Ites; Hittite, Jebuzite, etc., So, Abraham's most trusted servant stops at a well, and begins to pray to the God of his master, and was specific as to the type of woman. Yet God already had Isaac's wife picked out. He asked for a woman with a serving heart, essentially. As he was praying, a woman walks to the well to draw water and goes above and beyond what he requested. He then gave her gifts and asked for her father. Afterwards, they gathered to had a meal together. Abraham's most trusted servant told him why he was there and who sent him.

Abraham's most trusted servant's name was Eliezer; Rebekah was the woman who came to the well and did as Eliezer prayed for and more; Bethuel is the name of Rebekah's father. Eliezer means God's divine help or God is my help. Rebekah means to tie to, captivating beauty. Bethuel means house of God. So, Abraham sent God's divine help to the house of God to find a wife for Isaac.

A wife will cause a man to leave his father and mother and adjoin to his wife.

Just as God presented a wife to Adam, God did the same thing for Abraham's promised seed; just as God is doing right now for His Son, Jesus. This is a Christophany; a foreshadowing of Jesus and the Church.

Father God has chosen a Bride for His Son, Jesus.

She will be presented to Him at the marriage supper dressed in linen without spot or blemish - a glorious Bride. She will rule and reign with her Bridegroom.

> *Areas that break up marriages – Dr. Jamal-Harrison Bryant*
>
> 1. *Income*
> 2. *Intimacy (frequency, quality, quantity, fidelity). The bedroom is undefiled*
> 3. *Imagination (undiscussed expectations)*

When a woman marries a man, she takes on his last name and every privilege that comes with it. As the Bride of Christ (Church), we are covered under His name.

Jesus said, Whatsoever ye shall ask the Father in My name, He will give it you. (John 16:23b; 14:11-14)

> *"Don't expect anyone to be faithful to you if they aren't faithful to God."*
> *Pastor John F. Hannah*

Kingdom Covenant (Marriage) is about bringing God's Kingdom in the earth.

God is a God of order, not chaos, not confusion

God is a God of love, not evil, not hate

God is a God of peace, not war

God is a God of joy, not depression

God is a God of charity, not selfishness

God is a God of longsuffering (patience), not I gotta have it now

God is a God of temperance (self-control), not undisciplined

God is a God of meekness, not power hungry

God is a God of faith, not flakiness, non-dependable

Why do brides wear white? Many believe it is a sign of virginity.

In Revelations, the Bride of Christ will be presented to the Bridegroom in linen (or white); without spot or blemish. (Revelations 19:6-9)

You can wear white and be full of hell. It's about the inside, your heart, your soul.

Dressing holy does not make you holy.

You can learn how to be a wife.

Who washes dishes, takes out the garbage is earthly things. Yes, we must take care of home; however, that's not the focus. Satan wants you focused on mundane things, arguing over mundane things so you wouldn't focus on him, what he's doing.

Covenant, Kingdom Covenant, is heavenly things.

But first and most importantly, seek (aim at, strive after) His kingdom and His righteousness [His way of doing and being right—the attitude and character of God], and all these things will be given to you also. (Matthew 6:33 AMP)

Ask and keep on asking and it will be given to you; seek and keep on seeking and you will find; knock and keep on knocking and the door will be opened to you. For everyone who keeps on seeking finds, and to him who keeps on knocking, it will be opened. (Matthew 7:7-8 (AMP))

When man and woman stand at the altar before God to come into Covenant, that man and that woman come as a husband and a wife.

Ecclesiastes 4:9-12 9 Two are better than one; because they have a good reward for their labour. 10 For if they fall, the one will lift up his fellow; but woe to him that is alone when he falleth; for he hath not another to help him up. 11 Again, if two lie together, then they have heat; but how can one be warm alone? 12 And if one prevails against him, two shall withstand him; and a three-cord is not quickly broken

Satan knows your power better than you do. Satan knows you better than you do.

The garden of Eden was God's Kingdom in the earth. Satan recognized that. Keep in mind, Satan lived in Heaven. He was a part of God's Kingdom. The garden of Eden was another chance for him to rule and reign on God's throne.

You are a threat to Satan. Heaven is on your side. Satan knows that if everyone knew who Jesus is and who we are in Jesus his time would be up. He knows as long as we are divided, he gets to wreak havoc a little longer. Satan still attacks the same way. He does not have any new tricks.

This is a spiritual battle.

The wife brings the husband favor. Your husband is your covering. Would you curse who is covering you? Would you curse Jesus? Would you treat Jesus that way? Keep your mouth off your husband unless you're speaking life and blessings into and over his life.

As Apostle Paul says, there is no good thing in the flesh. He crucified the flesh daily. *For I know that in me (that is, my flesh) dwelleth no good thing: for to will is present with me; but how to perform that which is good I find not. 19 For the good that I would I do not; but the evil which I would not, that I do. 20 Now if I do that I would not, it is no more I that do it, but sin that dwelleth in me.* (Romans 7:18-20)

Then said Jesus unto His disciples, If any man will come after me, let him deny

himself, and take up his cross and follow me. (Matthew 16:24)

Galatians 5:16-26 *This I say then, Walk in the Spirit, and ye shall not fulfill the lust of the flesh. 17 For the flesh lusteth against the Spirit, and the Spirit against the flesh; and these are contrary to the other: so that ye cannot do things that we would. 18 But if ye be led of the Spirit, ye are not under the law. 19 Now the works of the flesh are manifest, which are these; Adultery, fornication, uncleanness, lasciviousness, 20 idolatry, witchcraft, hatred, variance, emulations, wrath, strife, seditions, heresies, 21 envyings, murders, drunkenness, revelings, and such like of the which I tell you before, as I have also told you in time past, that they which do such things shall not inherit the Kingdom of God. 22 But the fruit of the Spirit is love, joy, peace, longsuffering, gentleness, goodness, faith, 23 meekness, temperance: against such there is no law. 24 And they that are Christ's have crucified the flesh with the affections and lusts. 25 If we live in the Spirit, let us also walk in the Spirit. 26 Let us not be desirous of vain glory, provoking one another, envying one another.)*

Matthew 26:41 *Watch and pray, that ye enter not into temptation: the spirit indeed is willing, but the flesh is weak.*

You cannot pour out of an empty carton, glass, soul. You're human. Recognize it. Embrace it. Stay connected to the source, God's Kingdom. Do not feel guilty for saying, "No." You are supposed to be a living, breathing, walking, talking, tabernacle of the Holy Ghost.

Healed. Delivered. Whole. Casting all your cares upon Him for He cares for you.

When you come together, as a broken person, with someone who is also broken, that is twice the toxicity. You're actually in a relationship with the male version of you. You end up enabling each other, then no one gets made whole.

Are you truly born again? Have you truly given Jesus all your cares? Come to me all those that are heavy laden, I will give you rest. (Matthew 11:28-30)

Jeremiah 8:22 Is there no balm in Gilead; is there not a physician there? Why then is not the health of the daughter (Zion) of my people recovered?

1 Peter 5:7 casting all your cares upon Him; for He careth for you.

Baptism

Water is for purification. The fire of the Holy Ghost will burn up the chaff in your soul. Old things are passed away, behold all things are new. There is no more condemnation in Christ Jesus. You are a new creature in Christ Jesus. (Romans 8:1; 2 Corinthians 5:17)

Be not conformed to this world but be ye transformed by the renewing of your mind. (Romans 12:2)

Make sure you are a whole, healed, delivered, born-again believer before coming together with someone; do not even date. Allow God to do a perfect work in you. You can be as beautiful, fine, handsome, dressed well and be full of hell. Stop giving Satan credit and ammunition for what is going on inside of you. Seek the healer, Dr. Jesus. You must be made whole, then you will be introduced to someone who is whole.

The Lord God gives us grace to become who we are supposed to become.

Kingdom love is sacrificial, unconditional, intentional, on purpose, purposeful.

2 Corinthians 4:2 But have renounced the hidden things of dishonesty, not walking in craftiness, nor handling the Word of God deceitfully; but by manifestation of the truth commending ourselves to every man's conscience in the sight of God

What are you renouncing? Have you decided that you will start your marriage with a clean slate, so to speak? Have you ejected, rejected past hurts, pain, disappointments, relationships gone wrong because they weren't supposed to be, hurt, rejection, unforgiveness, bitterness, uncleanness? What are you bringing with you that you should not?

The flesh wars against the Spirit; the Spirit wars against the flesh. (Galatians 5:17; Matthew 26:4). What are you feeding? Your flesh? Your Spirit? (Galatians 6:8; 1 Peter 2:12) Know the difference between flesh and Spirit. He that sows to the flesh shall reap eternal damnation. He that sows to the spirit shall have eternal life. (Galatians 6:8)

Galatians 6:7-8 *Be not deceived; God is not mocked: for whatsoever a man soweth, that shall he also reap; 8 For he that soweth to the flesh shall of the flesh reap corruption; but he that soweth to the Spirit shall of the Spirit reap life everlasting*

Guard your heart, for out of it flows the issues of life. (Proverbs 4:23)

Who are you listening to? What are you listening to?

Who are you watching? What are you watching?

What are you reading?

What are you feeding you?

Will you sacrifice what is not of God?

Have you left your past in your past? God will **not** introduce you to your Kingdom husband until you allow Him to purge you from all uncleanness, ungodliness, remove all those skeletons from your closet.

Repent. Pray. Seek Deliverance (Renounce). Healing (Purging).

Speak the Word of God over and into your life.

Satan is here to steal, kill, and destroy by whatever means necessary. If he cannot kill you while in your mother's womb, he will find a way by attacking your identity – who you are, are you male or female; violence, perversion, slavery, divorce, idolatry, adultery, pride, arrogance, division, strife, anger, drugs, alcohol. If Satan controls your identity, he controls your life. Knowing who and whose you are is a must, not a maybe.

Dating

Dating is you looking. God didn't tell us to go out looking. He who finds a wife finds a good thing and receives favor from the Lord. Adam didn't go looking for Eve. God created Eve for Adam. He found her when God presented her to him. We don't choose God. God calls us. Our Father chooses the Bride for the Bridegroom. God already knows who is for who because He knows what He put in each of us for His purpose. He knows our hearts. We get the benefits. When we're out looking, dating, do we truly know what or who we're looking for? We have lists, preferences, non-negotiables, so on and so forth. What does that have to do with the Kingdom of God? Do you know who you are? Do you know what's in you? Do you know your purpose? Do you think your job, career, or work is your purpose? Are you passionate about what you do? Are you called to what you do? Do you know what's in you? How do you know what you're looking for? Will you know when you meet him? Your husband should be looking at a mirror reflection of himself, his purpose.

If you don't know who you are, your purpose, then how do you know what you're looking for?

Eve, get away from that tree.

Is it your spirit man looking? Or are you being led by your flesh? Covenant is Kingdom. Those who worship God must worship Him in Spirit and in Truth, not flesh. Flesh must be crucified daily. Flesh is your sin nature. Marriage does not correct what your flesh chose, it amplifies it more.

You have all these flesh marriages out there that grieves your spirit man, that you tied your spirit man to and wonder why the next relationship didn't work out. You've been committing adultery over and over again. You're like a polygamist.

Consecrate Yourself

Consecration is purification; you don't do anything with anyone; it's preparation for Kingdom Covenant. If God revealed to you who He has chosen to be your husband, you then will allow God to prepare you for that person; even if God has not yet revealed your husband, and your desire is to be married, you must still be prepared, consecrated. You don't date. You don't flirt. You are called. You are chosen. You are graced for that specific husband. God will teach you about, show you who he is, and the purpose for bringing the two of you together; if you listen to and allow God to do what He does. It's not easy. I can testify to that. I ran out of patience a few times. Like, when? Then God will show me something else I need to work on. I did not flirt. I did not date. I made sure I let the men who approached me know that I am not available. I am betrothed; God has already chosen my husband; that I am promised to someone already.

Eve, do you know who you are?

Declare things that are not as though they were. (Genesis 17:5; Romans 4:16-22)

Have you divorced your previous husband(s) in the Courts of Heaven? God is the Judge of Judges. He is the Just Judge. You may not have legally married that person, but you have sexual spiritual ties with him. Ask God to divorce you from that person(s). You are married by Biblical standards. You cannot take other people into your marriage, especially not a Kingdom Covenant. God will not allow it. There is no shame. There is no more condemnation in Christ Jesus. (Romans 8:1) Old things are passed away; behold all things are new. (2 Corinthians 5 14-21)

Guard your heart. Guard your peace. Forgive them but don't let them back in. Pray for them. Pray for God to bless them. Do not return evil for evil; reviling for reviling. Vengeance is mine, says the Lord; I will recompense. Don't give hurt, pain, disappointment a permanent residence in your soul. Renounce it. Forgive. Live.

When you were called out of the world, the world should have been left behind, so *DO NOT* take the concepts, systems of the world and try to blend it, marry it to the Word of God. Each of us should have divorced the world once we were called out. One cannot truly say I am born again, I am a new creature in Christ Jesus, yet try to blend, marry, if you will, the world to the Word of God. No. Be not conformed to the world, but be ye transformed by the renewing of your mind. We are supposed to be Christ-like, have the mind, heart, and ways of Jesus.

Otherwise, you are committing adultery against God. Yes, you can commit adultery against God. It's not just between husband and wife. "Thou shalt not commit adultery" is one of the commandments God gave in Exodus (20:14, cr Jeremiah 3:8). You're cheating on God with Satan. Adultery is a physical and emotional abandonment.

God will align you with the husband that would be called, chosen, graced for Kingdom Covenant.

Kingdom Covenant is a calling.

You are called

You are chosen

You are graced

You are equipped

...to be a specific man's wife.

There are women saying they are looking for or waiting on their "Boaz." Ruth followed the instructions of her mother-in-law. The first instruction Ruth received was to take off her mourning clothes. She was still mourning her husband that had died. Are you mourning the dead things: relationships, opportunities, etc.? Are you still wearing your "mourning clothes"? Boaz will walk right past you because he sees you're wearing "mourning clothes" and, out of respect, will not approach you.

While you're waiting on your "Boaz," are you preparing like Esther did to meet her King? Do you feel unworthy like the woman in Song of Solomon? *Are you bringing something to the table like the Proverbs 31 woman?*

There are times you have to go to God to keep from strangling your husband, your children, and whoever else done lost their ever loving mind.

"Daddy! Your son, get him, Lord, before I do. Daddy! Those kids I asked for, take them before I hurt them, Lord! Lord, how about you take me home and leave them here."

Pray before you speak. It's okay to be angry, but sin not. Do not let the sun set on your wrath. (Ephesians 4:26) In other words, do not hold onto your anger and let it simmer and pour out on the next day. The enemy will give you some thoughts, some suggestions on how you should handle your feelings. Do not let a temporary situation cause you to make a permanent decision.

Marriages have a cross whereas the flesh must be crucified in order to live out and walk in the principles of Kingdom Covenant. This isn't about who is supposed to cook, clean, take out the trash, or get up in the middle of the night for a crying baby or a child that got scared. This is about bringing God's Kingdom into the earth. The garden of Eden was God's Kingdom in the earth. There was order, peace, and harmony, not lack; everything was provided beforehand.

God will not send the wife to the husband unless there is provision. The wife will then multiply the provision because she brings God's favor, divine favor with her. (Be fruitful, multiply, and fill the earth).

Pastor Jentzen Franklin: a woman is a multiplier. When a man gives a woman his seed, she will multiply it and give him a baby. Give a woman a house and she will multiply it and make it a home. Give a woman trouble and she will multiply it, pressed down, shaken together, and running over, will she give it back to you. (LOL)

Just as God is preparing the Bride for the Bridegroom, God prepares his sons and daughters to be the Bridegrooms and the Brides. This is all preparation to reign with Christ Jesus. If you cannot reign together in the earth as husband and wife, how can you then reign with Christ Jesus?

The wife is woman, his womb. The wife is the female, the feminine to his masculine. A womb carries, gestates. Feminine is a soft place, a vulnerability. There's strength in a woman that makes hell nervous, demons flee.

Satan knows this and that's why he approached our Mother in the Garden. The seed of the woman shall crush his head. Abortion, prostitution, strip teasing, the chick on the side, plastic surgery; steal, kill, and destroy. She is God's favor to her husband.

As individuals, each of us has have a cross to bear; flesh to be crucified. You must crucify your flesh daily.

How is your prayer life? Do you have one? Life will give you a prayer life; trials and tribulations. If you're constantly quitting on God, what else are you or would you quit when it gets tough? Pray for each other. Sow into each other.

Love does not abandon ship. Love keeps the ship floating. The storms will rock and toss the ship. If you call on Jesus, speak peace be still, Jesus will get you through the storms as a single person. If you have a prayer life, Jesus is in the boat with you. The Holy Ghost that dwells in you and with you will guide you through or around the storms. *If there are disciples, children, your relationship with your husband must be united, strong.* Your family is a strong as your Covenant with each other. *Action speaks louder than words. I can show you better than I can tell you.* Love is action. Love does when feelings won't. *Your children are your disciples.* If you do not have a prayer life, you will set the course of dysfunction for generations. God is a God of generations. He doesn't just look at (consider) you. He looks at Abraham, Isaac, and Jacob.

2 Corinthians 6:14-15 Be ye not unequally yoked together with unbelievers: for what fellowship hath righteousness with unrighteousness? And what communion hath light with darkness? 15 and what concord hath Christ with Belial? Or what part hath he that believeth with an infidel?

Unevenly yoked: there are times God will have a Believer joined to an Unbeliever…for His purpose. God knows that the Believer will pray for, speak into the Unbeliever. God has plans for that Unbeliever. So, God will bring a Believer and an Unbeliever together; and the Believer will represent the Love of God to the Unbeliever. The Believer will cause the Unbeliever to seek God because of the Love of God in the Believer and flowing through the Believer.

There are times where God will remove an Unbeliever from the Believer's life because that Unbeliever is a hindrance to the Believer's destiny, purpose God has for that Believer.

God will remove people, places, and things out of the life of the Believer. When God sees that the Believer is still chasing after, longing for him, the things and the places, God will remove the person, places, and things even further from the Believer's grasp, from the Believer's life.

That's why certain relationships did not work out, personal and business. That's why you cannot get a loan or credit. That's why you are not able to go to certain places.

God sees and knows the end from the beginning. We quote it but do we believe it, truly believe it? That is called being in the will of the Father. Stop blaming everything on the devil. The safest and wisest place to be is in the will of God. There is turmoil, chaos outside of God's will.

We say we're waiting on God for a car or a new car. We say we're waiting on God for a house. We say we're waiting on God for a financial miracle. I'm waiting on God for healing. I don't hear many say, "I'm waiting on God for my husband."

Are you allowing God to prepare you for your husband?

What are you doing while you're waiting?

Where two or three are gathered in His name, there He shall be in the midst.

Where two are touching and agreeing on a thing. (Matthew 18:19-20)

God has given each person purpose. When God aligns people, places, and things, it is to fulfill your God-given purpose. Your purpose, primarily, is to bring God's Kingdom into the earth.

When you allow God to choose, you are in the Spirit.

It is not about what your flesh wants. It's about the Kingdom of Heaven.

Even Believers can be unequally yoked.

You cannot marry just anyone. If that person does not have the missing ingredients to your purpose, then what God has purposed for you will not be whole; your purpose will be delayed; there will be friction constantly; it will feel like the gates of hell is in your home.

The person you want to be with so bad may have the ingredients to make pizza, but you need the rest of the ingredients to make a cake. That person has the cheese and the dough, but you need sugar and vanilla extract and perhaps a pinch of salt; and a stick of butter. He needs the tomato sauce and seasoning, and you have flour, eggs, milk, a stick of butter, and a pinch of salt. You will not like the taste of that pizza when you put the ingredients you have together with the ingredients that person has and surely not the taste of that cake.

God knows what you need and when you need it. The oven has to be preheated. You may even need the right oven first and the right pans and the mixer.

We're always saying, "I'm waiting on God."

What does that mean? Are you sitting around somewhere doing nothing?

What are you doing while you're "waiting"? Are you allowing God to do a work on the inside of you?

God sees the beginning from the end. He already knows what is going to happen. That's why Jesus was the Lamb slain before the foundations of the World.

Love on purpose, for a purpose, intentionally.

Knowing who and whose you are will absolutely change your life. You cannot have healthy relationships when you're not healthy; mind, heart, spirit, and body.

Beloved, I wish above all things that thou mayest prosper and be in health, even as your soul prosper (3 John v2)

(AMP) says, "good health [physically] just as I know your soul prospers [spiritually]

Ye present your bodies a living sacrifice, holy, acceptable unto God, which is your reasonable service (Romans 12:1)

Know ye not, that ye are the temple of God, and that the Spirit of God dwelleth in you (1 Corinthians 3:16)

Once you truly know who and whose you are, your choices will change; what and who you listen to, watch will change; your walk will change, your talk will change; your vision will change, your perspective will change; all things become new because you are a new creation in Christ Jesus. (2 Corinthians 5:17)

You become more and more like Christ. And the two shall become one. Bridegroom and His Bride. Husband and wife. When you see me, you see Jesus. When you see my husband, you see me. I am Christ-like in deed and in name. All that He is, I am.

You cannot, dare not love your husband with your flesh. That's not Kingdom. That's the world. In this flesh is no good thing. Seek your husband in the Spirit and it will manifest in the natural. You should choose to be his Aaron and Ur when necessary. Choose to war in the Spirit against every ungodly attack. Choose to speak life, love, joy, peace, strength and you will see it manifest in the natural. Choose to love him unconditionally, sacrificially, intentionally, purposefully, on purpose. This is not about your feelings. Feelings are fickle. Feelings are temporary. Pray before speaking or taking action on anything; even if it's from your husband. Hug him. Pray for him. Do not respond in kind. That old saying, "Two wrongs don't make a right." Pray. Pray. Pray. Pray. Pray. Pray. I cannot say that enough. Pray. Forgive. That's a MUST. Do NOT give the enemy an opening. Do NOT give the enemy an opening. Do NOT give the enemy an opening. Repeat: I will NOT give the enemy an opening.

1 Corinthians 7:2-5
> 1b It is good for a man not to touch a woman

> 2 Nevertheless, to avoid fornication, let every man have his own wife, and let every woman have her own husband

> 3 Let the husband render unto the wife due benevolence; and likewise, also the wife unto the husband

> 4 The wife hath not power of her own body, but the husband: and likewise, also the husband hath not power of his own body, but the wife

> 5 Defraud ye not one the other, except it be with consent for a time, that ye may give yourselves to fasting and praying; and come together again, that Satan tempt you not for your incontinency

When husband and wife are standing at the altar, facing the Priest/Pastor who will speak the words to join the husband and wife together, what are you agreeing to do? Who is this Covenant with? After you say, "I do," are you taking God with you? Or are you leaving Him at the altar? Was He invited?

There will be days where you will need God the Father, God the Son, and God the Holy Ghost.

Psalm 127:1 Except the Lord build the house, they labor in vain that build it; except the Lord keep the city, the watchman waketh but in vain.

In order to give a description of a wife, who a wife is, and her responsibilities, so to speak, we must see and understand what and who is a husband. When God created the first wife, the 1st Adams wife, God put Adam to sleep, cut open his side, removed a rib, closed his side, then created a creature and presented this creature to Adam; just as God did with all the other creatures. However, this creature was created using a part of Adam. Let's look at that part and what that part signifies. The rib cage itself has double duty, if you will. It gives the upper torso shape; thus, allowing vital organs to function properly and gives those organs protection along with the sinew, the muscle, and some fat. Scripture says, God opened Adam's side, yes; indicating Adam's wife is to be at his side. God did not remove a bone from Adam's back, buttocks, nor feet. Unfortunately, that's how God's daughters have been positioned and treated. It's indoctrinated in manmade cultures, not God's Kingdom. Amen.

When God presented this creature, like all other creatures God created, Adam proclaimed, "Bone of my bones, flesh of my flesh; you shall be called Woman because you came out of Man." Then, God proclaimed, "A wife will cause a man to leave thy father and thy mother and cleave to his wife, and the twain shall become one. The wife is her husband's rib. Adam did not go looking for a wife. God saw a need only a wife can fulfill; her husband's purpose. God has always given gifts to his daughters. What are yours? Are you using your God-given, God-purposed gifts? Do you know what's inside of you? What are your God-given dreams, visions?

Virtuous Woman

The Virtuous woman (Proverbs 31 wife) got up while her husband and children still slept and got before God. Ladies, you need your own prayer life. You have to go to war at times for your husband, for your children; and at times for your parents, siblings, nieces, nephews, and friends. There are times you have to go to God to keep from strangling your husband, your children and whoever else done lost their ever loving mind. Daddy! Your son, get him, Lord, before I do. Daddy! Those kids I asked for, take them before I hurt them, Lord! Lord, how about you take me home and leave them here.

God will bring together two imperfect people who will love each other as God loves us; will see each other as God sees us.

A few thousand years ago, there was this woman called the Proverbs 31 woman.

When did the woman become the property of the man? When did she become sex tools, sex idols, made to sell her body, walk around half naked to catch a man?

An Unruly Wife Is Like...

Proverbs 19:13-14 (Tanakh) A stupid son is a calamity to his father; The nagging of a wife is like endless dripping of water 14 Property and riches are bequeathed by fathers, But an efficient wife comes from the Lord

(KJV) A foolish son is the calamity of his father; and the contentions of a wife are a continual dropping 14 House and riches are the inheritance of fathers; and a prudent wife is from the Lord

Proverbs 21:19 (Tanakh) It is better to live in the desert than with a contentious, vexatious wife

(KJV) It is better to dwell in the wilderness, than with a contentious and an angry woman

Proverbs 19:9 (Tanakh) Dwelling in the corner of a roof is better than a contentious wife in a spacious house

(KJV) It is better to dwell in a corner of the housetop, than with a brawling woman in a wide house

A Gracious Wife/Woman Is Like

Proverbs 11:16 (Tanakh) A graceful woman obtains honor; ruthless men obtain wealth

(KJV) A gracious woman retaineth honour; and strong men retain riches

Proverbs 14:1 (Tanakh) The wisest of women builds her house, but folly tears it down with its own hands

(KJV) Every wise woman builds her house; but the foolish plucketh it down with her hands

How can God bring two people together less they agree? Why do we wait until an engagement to learn who we are and our purpose as Kingdom Covenant partners, so to speak? Do you know what it means to be the Bride of Christ? Do you know what Covenant means?

There are going to be issues in God's house and our own houses. You are the Church. Wherever you go, there's the Church. We do not leave the Church behind after Sunday services or Bible Study. What to do and how to run your household, you learn in God's house from your Pastor by the Word of God; and by your own studying, reading, and meditating on the Word of God.

God's love is sacrificial, unconditional, intentional, on purpose, and purposeful.

Love is not about how I feel at any given moment to decide what I should do or be doing. Love is a decision. Love is responsibility. Love is choosing to be responsible for how you talk to, do for, treat, how you make the object, the person, feel. Regardless of how you feel, love does. Love does not hold back giving, doing. That's what the world does. Kingdom love is sacrificial, unconditional, intentional, on purpose, purposeful.

When you choose what your flesh wants, you'll get hell.

Prepare like Esther

Rub oils into your skin, get your hair done, or do it yourself, get your mani and pedi. Don't go out in public looking like you're about to clean your home. Esther wasn't introduced to the king until after she was prepared. Oils and perfumes were applied, of course, after being bathed. There were probably oils in the bath water. Men are carnal creatures. We first glean with our natural eyes. Adam and Eve were naked and unashamed together.

Honor like Ruth

Wherever you go, I will go. Your people shall be my people. Your God shall be my God. Where you die, I shall die. Boaz noticed Ruth while she was gleaning the fields. She was working to bring home food for her and her mother in law. Boaz heard of her reputation; how she left behind all she knew, her family and her home, a familiar place; a familiar people, familiar gods.

Pray as bold as Hannah

What Hannah sacrificed to God, God gave back to her five times. God accepted her sacrifice and blessed her. Pray bold and be willing to sacrifice.

<u>Go to war like Deborah</u>

<u>Expect the impossible like Sarai</u>

<u>Sit at Jesus' feet like Mary</u>

Keep in mind....

Marriage does not correct the mess you made with your loins. Fornication is not solved by marrying that person. The mess you made only gets amplified.

Years down the road, you'll be trying to figure out what happened. You chose with your loins, your lust. Then, you're telling everybody God blessed you with this person. You realized after you said, "I do" that you really didn't hear from God. It was your flesh, your lusts. Now what? Do you continue to perpetuate the fraud? Or do you confess you were wrong as to who you listened to? Did God really say?

If the man that asked you to marry him says to you, "you won't get far without me" "I have all the connections," for example. That's not your husband. That's a warlock. Manipulation is witchcraft. He's not of God or from God.

If you move forward, he becomes your god. Now you're in idolatry and adultery. That man has become your idol, hence idolatry. You put that man before God, thus, you've committed adultery.

God doesn't say choose me or else. God says choose me because I love you. I want you to have life and have it more abundantly. I want you to live with me forever. There will be peace on earth. There will be no peace in that marriage. You will be in bondage.

God sees what attracts you. God knows what attracts you. And so does Satan because you tell him with your words and show him by your actions. God will prepare you, then introduce you to who He chose for you. Satan will parade the imitation in your face until you give in.

God will put an open book test before you. You put the Word of God on that test. Satan will keep coming, sending imitations waiting for you to fail. It's not a multiple choice test. The answer is the Word. So, are you going to put the Word on the test? Or choose with your flesh? Yes, you still have a choice. You can align with God or choose your flesh. Flesh is your sin nature. God is Spirit. Are you going to walk with God? Or go the way of the world, which is Satan?

Do not allow a temporary season of being single, where you feel loneliness and just anybody is better than nobody. You'll find yourself 10, 15, 20, 25 years down the road trying to figure out what you were thinking, looking at each other upside the head. Then, you decide to stay because you don't want to start over or be alone. Some of you will choose to hold onto that person because you poured so much into that person. You don't want somebody else to benefit from it. Seriously?! Then, you try to make that person your identured servant, slave, until they work off whatever that person owe you. Seriously?! I know it's true. I said once that I didn't want another woman benefitting from my hard work. I was building an organization, and if he was cheating on me, or things just didn't work out, that heifer wasn't going to be in my face smiling, benefitting from my hard work. Then I grew up in Jesus.

You don't own anyone. You don't even own yourself. Learn from it. Grow up in Jesus from it. Life will give you lessons. You were bought with a price; the blood of Jesus.

PRAYERS

Lord God, I renounce sin, trespasses, iniquities in the name of Jesus.

Lord God, I renounce fornication, adultery, idolatry, masturbation, bitterness, anger, hate in the name of Jesus.

Lord God, I renounce unforgiveness, envy, jealousy, pride, arrogance in the name of Jesus.

Lord God, I renounce murder, division, strife, excessive alcohol, wine, spirits, eating in the name of Jesus.

Lord God, I renounce smoking, drugs in the name of Jesus.

Lord God, as my heavenly Father, I ask that you break every vow I made knowingly and unknowingly that is contrary to Your Word and purpose for my life in the name of Jesus.

Lord God, I ask You to divorce me from my spiritual husband(s) in the name of Jesus.

Lord God, I ask You to teach me what I should be eating and drinking so that I may prosper and be in good health as my soul prospers in the name of Jesus.

Lord God, I receive Your love for me, Your peace that passes all understanding, Your joy that is unspeakable in the name of Jesus.

Lord God, I ask You to heal my soul, body and renew in me a right spirit in Jesus name.

Lord God, I want to be whole that I may be of service to Your Kingdom in the name of Jesus.

Lord God, I ask You to baptize me with Your Holy Spirit in the name of Jesus; that I will walk in Your ways, speak Your ways in the name of Jesus, so I may hear Your heart in the name of Jesus.

All these things I pray in the name of Jesus Christ.

Amen. Amen. Amen.

Lord, I speak to those natural and spiritual gifts You put in Your daughter while she was yet formed in her mother's womb. In the name of Jesus, arise, wake-up gifts; be fruitful, multiply and fill the earth; not by might, not by power, by the Spirit of the Lord; take your place in the earth; you shall thrive and live out your Kingdom purpose, in the name of Jesus Christ; it is so and so it is.

Amen. Amen. Amen.

Husband and Wife

What is their purpose? Who are they?

Chapter 5

Chapter 5 | Husband and Wife

        J
        E
        S
        U
        S

H U S B A N D AND W I F E

        C
        H
        I
        L
        D
        R
        E
        N

"Don't expect anyone to be faithful to you if they aren't faithful to God."

-Pastor John F. Hannah

Take your rightful place, thus saith the Lord.

Adam, do you know who you are?

Eve, do you know who you are?

The old, rugged cross is our engagement ring.

This time on earth is our engagement period before the wedding supper.

We are in preparation for the upcoming wedding.

Genesis

1:26 God said, Let us make man in our image, after our likeness: and let them have dominion over the fish of the sea, and over the fowl of the ear, over the cattle, and over all the earth, and over every creeping thing that creepeth upon the earth

1:27 So God created man in His own image, in the image of God created He him; male and female created He them

1:28 And God blessed them, and God said unto them, Be fruitful, and multiply, and replenish the earth, and subdue it; and have dominion over the fish of the sea, and over the fowl of the air, and over every living thing that moveth upon the earth

1:29 And God said, Behold, I have given you every herb bearing seed, which is upon the face of all the earth, and every tree, in which is the fruit of a tree yielding seed; to you it shall be for meat

2:7 And the Lord God formed man of the dust of the ground, and breathed into his nostrils the breath of life; and man became a living soul

2:8 And the Lord God planted a garden eastward of Eden; and there he put the man whom he had formed

2:15 And the Lord God took the man, and put him into the garden of Eden to dress it and to keep it.

2:16 And the Lord God commanded the man, saying, Of every tree of the garden thou mayest freely eat:

2:17 But of the tree of the knowledge of good and evil, thou shalt not eat of it: for in the day that thou eatest thereof thou shalt surely die

2:18 And the Lord God said, It is not good that the man should be alone; I will make him an help meet for him

2:19 And out of the ground the Lord God formed every beast of the field, and every fowl of the air; and brought them unto Adam to see what he would call them: and whatsoever Adam called every living creature, that was the name thereof

2:20 And Adam gave names to all cattle, and to the fowl of the air and t every beast oof the field; but for Adam there was not found an help meet for him.

2:21 the Lord God caused a deep sleep to fall upon Adam, and he slept; and He took one of his ribs, and closed up the flesh; the rib, which the Lord God had taken from Man, made He a woman, and brought her unto the Man

2:22 And the rib, which The Lord God had taken from man, made he a woman, and brought her unto the man

2:23 Adam said this is now bone of my bones, and flesh of my flesh; she shall be called Woman because she came out of man

Genesis

2:24 Therefore shall a man leave his father and mother, and shall cleave unto his wife: and they shall be one flesh

2:25 And they were both naked; the man and his wife; and were not ashamed.

When God reached into the earth, as we would like to envision, and formed Man (Adam) then breathed the breath of life into Man and Man became a living soul. Male and female were together as one.

God provided everything for Man before creating Man. God saw man and knew what man would need, from the beginning to the end. Alpha and Omega. The Beginning and The End. There will be seed time and harvest. God sowed into us before we were born.

When God created Man (Adam), and placed the Man in the garden of Eden they were one. God then took the female out of male, the woman out of the man, and put the femininity and womb into a creature then presented her to Adam. What God took out of the man (male), He put in the woman (female). And that's why he recognized his bone, his flesh; and declared bone of my bones, flesh of my flesh.

How did Adam know where that woman came from? It was spiritual. Before God created a wife for Adam, God gave Adam the responsibility of naming all the creatures and tending the garden of Eden. In other words, God gave Adam a job before creating a wife. God also gave Adam instructions, commandments of what to do and not to do.

God gave Man (Adam) dominion. The first Man (Adam) disobeyed and gave dominion to Satan. So, God sent His Son in the form of flesh to take dominion back.

Jesus is called the last Adam (Man).

Kingdom Covenant expressed by a marriage: the responsibility of the wife and the responsibility of the husband

Ephesians 5:22-33

> 22 Wives, submit yourselves unto your own husbands, as unto the Lord
>
> 23 For the husband is the head of the wife, even as Christ is the head of the church: and he is the savior of the body
>
> 24 Therefore as the church is subject unto Christ, so let the wives be to their own husbands in everything.
>
> 25 Husbands, love your wives, even as Christ also loved the church, and gave himself for it.
>
> 26 That he might sanctify and cleanse it with the washing of water by the word,
>
> 27 That he might present it to himself a glorious church, not having spot, or wrinkle, or any such thing; but that it should be holy and without blemish.
>
> 28 So ought men to love their wives as their own bodies. He that loveth his wife loveth himself.
>
> 29 For no man ever yet hated his own flesh; but nourisheth and cherisheth it, even as the Lord the church:
>
> 30 For we are members of his body, of his flesh, and of his bones.
>
> 31 For this cause shall a man leave his father and mother, and shall be joined unto his wife, and they two shall be one flesh.

32 This is a great mystery: but I speak concerning Christ and the church.

33 Nevertheless let every one of you in particular so love his wife even as himself,; and the wife see that she reverence her husband.

This is about restoring Man to his rightful place. This is about preparing to reign with Jesus. This is what all the fuss is about, to put it plainly. We have already won and we must fight to keep it. Our parents, who are called Adam and Eve, were a foreshadowing of the Bridegroom and His Bride; Jesus and the Church.

God said the husband and wife shall become one (united) forsaking all others.

Jesus told those who wanted to follow Him that they must forsake father, mother, brother, and sister in order to follow Him. Jesus must be first. (Luke 14:25-35)

Verse 22, Submission is made into a dirty word. Being submitted to Christ Jesus has mind-blowing benefits. If a woman is not submitted to Christ Jesus, she will not be able to submit to her husband. If the husband is not submitted to Jesus, then what would his wife be submitted to?

Husbands, don't allow Satan to use you to bind your wife. You bind divine favor when you do that. God resists the proud and arrogant. How do you think God feels about how you treat His daughter? *Jesus' ministry was supported by wealthy women.* Jesus freed, loosed women. It is man's pride and ego that puts and want to keep women in bondage.

If the husband and the wife, as the Church, are submitted to Christ Jesus, then they're both on a mission. Husbands, men, do not abuse that word.

Husbands, are you submitted to Christ Jesus? If the husband's will is not submitted to the Father, what will the wife be submitted to? The husband's flesh. With that scenario, God's Kingdom cannot be done in earth. The prince (ruler) of darkness runs that marriage. The husband's *will* is to be submitted to the Father, just like Jesus, as does the wife's will. Jesus' *will* was and is submitted to the Father.

Jesus is submitted to the Father. Everything that was made was made for Jesus. Our Father made everything for His Son. So, what's wrong with submission? Submission isn't slavery. Submission isn't about control, dictatorship. The woman is the rib of a man. The rib is not under his foot, behind his back; it's at his side. A husband's love for his wife commands her to submit, not demand.

Love is commanding, not demanding. If you are demanding things to be done your way, that is not love. Demanding is control, mostly by a manipulative form of control; i.e., If you don't do this, I will not do that. I'm not going to talk to you, do for you, if you don't do this or that for me.

God is not in that.

Submission is a powerful position to be in. Seek ye first the Kingdom of God and His righteousness, and all these things shall be added to you. There are benefits to being submitted to Jesus, and this is just the engagement stage.

The Church is supposed to be submitted to Christ Jesus. The Church is His Bride. The Church is His rib. The Church is supposed to be joint heirs with Jesus; to reign with Jesus. Yes?

Just as Jesus said, if you see Me, you see My Father; My Father and I are one.

The Church should be able to say that same thing; if you see me, you see Jesus, for Jesus and I are one.

We are to be naked and unashamed with the Bridegroom, as it was from the beginning. This is spiritual. Jesus knows everything, yet He wants you to be able to be open with Him; to have an intimate relationship with Him where you can tell your deepest secrets, deepest hurts, deepest desires, and be unashamed.

In Christ Jesus, there is no more condemnation (Romans 8:1)

Our Bridegroom sacrificed Himself for us; me, you.

Now that's love – sacrificial, unconditional, intentional, on purpose, purposeful.

1 Corinthians 11:3 But I would have you to know, that the head of every man is Christ; and the head of every woman is the man; and the head of Christ is God.

Verses 25-26 The husband is to be like the Bridegroom: Sacrificial, sanctifying, cleansing with the washing of water by the Word of God; nourishing, cherishing.

Husbands, speak the Word of God into your wife, over your wife.

Chapter 5 | Husband and Wife

Isaiah 55:11 So shall My word be that goeth forth out of My mouth, it shall not return unto Me void; but it shall accomplish that which I please, and it shall prosper in the thing whereto I sent it.

When the soldier pierced Jesus' side, out came water and blood, the water to purify and the blood to redeem Man. Just as God put the man Adam to sleep to remove a rib to create woman, then present this creature to the man, who then declares, "Bone of my bones, flesh of my flesh; you shall be called woman because you came out of man." Therefore, shall a wife cause a man to leave his father and mother and cleave to his wife; and the two shall become one. Jesus will declare that at the marriage supper.

The Word of God is to sanctify and purify the Church, Jesus' Bride.

The first man Adam blamed God for the woman God gave him.

The last man Adam, Jesus, died for His Bride; His side pierced for her. The water and blood that came out of His side to purify and redeem her.

This is Kingdom Covenant; the Bridegroom sacrificing, covering His Bride. His Bride becoming one with her Bridegroom in submission and reverence.

Apostle Paul stated in verse 33 that the wife is to reverence her husband. Reverence means to be in "awe." He sent redemption unto His people: He hath commanded His covenant forever; holy and reverend is His name. Reverend means to have a deep respect. (Psalm 111:9) The wife is to be like the Bride of Christ; submitted to Christ the Bridegroom; reverencing her husband.

Most of the instructions and commandments are given to the husband. Why? Because Jesus paid it all at the cross. The wife is to submit her will and to respect her husband. Sounds simple, easy; yet if the husband loves and leads like Jesus, the wife should not have any issues with submission.

Christ Jesus, the Lamb of God, slain before the foundations of the world, went to the cross to redeem mankind. The first Adam blamed the fall on God, saying it was that woman You gave me. The last Adam, Jesus, as He was hung high on a cross, stretched wide, arms wide open, said, I will die for her. I'll take her. His side was pierced just like the first man Adam. Jesus died for His Bride; out came water and blood to purify and redeem His Bride. Out of Jesus, His Bride was birthed. Most of the instructions are given to the Bridegroom because it was God the Father, Son, and Holy Ghost that decided this was how Man was to be redeemed. Jesus cried on that cross, "It is finished." What was finished? EVERYTHING.

It's the Word of God that washes us clean. Jesus is the Word of God.

How can we reign with Jesus if we do not know how to reign in the earth?

Reigning is about order, justice, peace, love, joy, charity, prosperity.

The first Adam did not redeem his bride; *because Our Mother allowed the devil to trick her and then give the forbidden fruit to our Father.* He could not because he disobeyed God and ate of the tree. Because Jesus obeyed God, He was able to redeem His Bride, as the last Adam.

Because our Father and Mother disobeyed God, sin entered into the world where there was no sin. That sinful nature passed down to their children, us. The sins of the father. Because Jesus did not sin, we were redeemed.

Because of sin, we were separated from God. Because of Jesus' obedience to the cross, we can go boldly to the throne of Grace and seek mercy. (Hebrews 4:16)

Man doesn't choose his wife. God our Father does. Jesus doesn't choose. The Father does. His Bride will be presented to Him at the marriage supper.

God created Covenant, not mankind. This is about the Kingdom of God. This is about bringing His Kingdom into the earth through the husband and wife.

You are limiting God by relegating marriage to having children and working; arguing over who's going to clean the house; take out the garbage; the roles of the husband and wife. That is the world's idea of what marriage is about. Marriage is a Kingdom Covenant between God, the husband, and wife. The husband is the Priest in the home, as Jesus is the High Priest of the Church. The wife is joint heir and is representative of the Church.

If you live, walk in Kingdom Principles, wives will not ask their husbands if he took out the trash; husbands will not ask their wives if they picked up the dry cleaning.

The world teaches that the woman takes care of the children, cooks, cleans, grocery shop, do laundry, gets the mail, have her husband's slippers ready when he comes home, keeps the kids away and quiet until he winds down from the day. The husband works to provide for his family and takes out the trash, perhaps mow the lawn, if you have one.

Marriages have a cross whereas the flesh must be crucified in order to live out and walk in the principles of Kingdom Covenant.

This isn't about who is supposed to cook, clean, take out the trash, or get up in the middle of the night for a crying baby or a child that got scared.

This is about bringing God's Kingdom into the earth.

The garden of Eden was God's Kingdom in the earth. There was order, peace, harmony, no lack; everything was provided beforehand.

We were created to reign in the earth. We were born to reign in the earth.

The Apostle Paul said it like this: we are joint heirs with Christ Jesus. (Romans 8:17)

Husband and wife were created to reign together in the earth.

Our Father and Mother (Adam and Eve) were created to reign in the earth. God gave Man dominion in the earth. Our disobedience gave Satan dominion. Jesus took dominion back when Satan used Man to crucify Him; crushing Satan's head.

Abraham tasks his most faithful servant, Eliezer to go to his hometown to find a wife for Isaac.

When Abraham's wife Sarah died, and Isaac was 40 y.o., Abraham called his most trusted servant to find a wife for Issac. (Genesis 24). He had him swear not to look upon any of the Ites; Hittite, Jebuzite, etc., So, Abraham's most trusted servant stops at a well, and begins to pray to the God of his master, and was specific as to the type of woman. Yet God already had Isaac's wife picked out. He asked for a woman with a serving heart, essentially. As he was praying, a woman walks to the well to draw water and goes above and beyond what he requested. He then gave her gifts and asked for her father. Afterwards, they gathered to had a meal together. Abraham's most trusted servant told him why he was there and who sent him.

Abraham's most trusted servant's name was Eliezer; Rebekah was the woman who came to the well and did as Eliezer prayed for and more; Bethuel is the name of Rebekah's father. Eliezer means God's divine help or God is my help. Rebekah means to tie to, captivating beauty. Bethuel means house of God. So, Abraham sent God's divine help to the house of God to find a wife for Isaac.

A wife will cause a man to leave his father and mother and adjoin to his wife.

Just as God presented a wife to Adam, God did the same thing for Abraham's promised seed; just as God is doing right now for His Son, Jesus. This is a Christophany; a foreshadowing of Jesus and the Church.

It's about the Kingdom of God. Satan's whole agenda is to destroy marriages. Let me clarify that; marriage is between a male and female. Adam and Eve.

Let's not forget about the journey to the Cross. Let's not forget about all that Jesus endured those 3½ years at the hands of the religious leaders. They were prideful, arrogant, jealous, and envious. Our husbands walk that journey as well. Why? Because the enemy is out to steal, kill, and destroy.

Just like Satan used our Mother to cause our Father to disobey God in the garden, Satan had been removed from Heaven because of the iniquity in his heart; our Father and Mother were removed from the garden of Eden, Heaven in the earth, because of sin.

Satan still attacks the same way. He does not have any new tricks. This is a spiritual battle.

What we do in the earth is all preparation to reign with the King of Kings, the Lord of Lords. We are supposed to bring God's Kingdom in the earth through us, through Covenant. This is on the job training (OJT) to reign with Jesus. There is a saying, "It's you and I against the world." It's certainly husband and wife against Satan.

We are destined to reign alongside the Bridegroom. We are supposed to be bone of his bones, flesh of his flesh. His rib. His Bride. If we're not doing in the earth now, reigning that is, understanding and operating in our purpose; then how are we to reign with Jesus when it's time?

We must understand our role here right now in the earth. Understanding and operating in Kingdom Covenant is very important. God is a God of love, order, justice, peace, joy, charity, patience, forgiveness, faithfulness, mercy, favor, wrath.

Kingdom Covenant is about Restoration. When Jesus came into the earth, it was for a purpose. He came for His Bride. He came to restore that which was lost. Kingship. Lordship. This has all been about Restoration. You are supposed to be living, breathing, walking, talking, tabernacles of the Holy Ghost.

The Covenant between husbands and wives are a microcosm of Jesus and His Church.

2 Corinthians 6:14-15 Be ye not unequally yoked together with unbelievers: for what fellowship hath righteousness with unrighteousness? And what communion hath light with darkness? 15 and what concord hath Christ with Belial? Or what part hath he that believeth with an infidel?

Unequally yoked: there are times God will have a Believer joined to an Unbeliever…for His purpose. God knows that the Believer will pray for, speak into the Unbeliever. God has plans for that Unbeliever. So, God will bring a Believer and an Unbeliever together; and the Believer will represent the Love of God to the Unbeliever. The Believer will cause the Unbeliever to seek God because of the Love of God in the Believer and flowing through the Believer.

There are times where God will remove an Unbeliever from the Believer's life because that Unbeliever is a hindrance to the Believer's destiny, purpose God has for that Believer.

Even Believers can be unequally yoked.

Kingdom Covenant is a calling.

You are called

You are chosen

You are graced

You are equipped

...to be a specific man's wife. He is your husband, no one else's. You are no one else's wife. You are that man's wife.

...to be a specific woman's husband. She is your wife, no one else's, yours. You are her husband, no one else's, her husband.

Why did God bring you two together? What vision did God give the husband?

What vision did God give the wife? How do those visions align? Education, Skills,

Giftings (spiritual and natural), Legacy building, Kinsmen Redeemer.

Man is made in the image and after the likeness of God.

In order for your Kingdom Covenant, marriage, to be fruitful, the husband and wife must be fruitful.

Marriage is a Ministry and Ministry is warfare. Ministry will wear you out. Take care of you first. We must cover one another in prayer. When the husband isn't at 100%, the wife must be at 130% or even 200%. When the wife isn't at 100%, the husband must be at 130% or even 200%. Take time off to rest. Get away. God forbid anything happens to your wife or your husband, whether its minor warfare or life-threatening. Your wife should be able to stand in the gap. Your husband should be able to stand in the gap.

Ecclesiastes 4:9-12 (AMP)

9 Two are better than one; because they have a more satisfying return for their labour; 10 for if either of them falls, the one will lift up his companion. But woe to him who is alone when he falls and does not have another to lift him up. 11 Again, if two lie down together, they keep warm: but how can one be warm alone? 12 And though one can overpower him who is alone, two can resist him. A cord of three strands is not quickly broken.

The cord of three strands represents God, the groom, and the bride – braiding these three strands symbolizes the joining of one man, one woman, and God in marriage. (Husband, wife, God in Covenant) By keeping the Lord at the center of marriage, His love will continue to grow and bind the couple together. That reminds me of a song lyric, "Lord, bind us together in love."

Binding and Loosing

What are you binding and loosing into your Kingdom Covenant? What are husbands and wives binding and loosing into their marriage? Into their family?

Matthew 18:19-20
> 19. Again I say unto you, That if two of you shall agree on earth as touching anything that they shall ask, it shall be done for them of my Father which is in Heaven.
>
> 20. For where two or three are gathered together in my name, there am I in the midst of them.

What are you touching and agreeing on as husband and wife? What are you binding and loosing into your marriage? Into your family?

What are you speaking into your marriage? What are you decreeing?

What are you loosing into your marriage?

What are you allowing or not allowing?

Death and life are in the power of the tongue, and those who love it and indulge it will eat its fruit and bear the consequences of their words. (Proverbs 18:21, AMP)

God decreed a thing and it was so. Let there be.

Where two or three are gathered in His name, He shall be in the midst. Husband, wife, and children. (Matthew 18:20) That's why Satan fights marriages, fights family.

Husbands, lead and love like Jesus. Understand the purpose of the Covenant. Understand the vision, the mission of the Covenant. Write it down, after speaking to your wife. She has what is needed to help bring that vision into manifestation, into fruition in the earth. If you bring children into the Covenant, come together as a family; where two or three are gathered in My name, saith the Lord, there shall I be in the midst. (Matthew 18:20) If you do not have children, yet plan on bringing children into the Covenant, where two touch and agree on a thing, it shall be done. (Matthew 18:19 v18) Our children are our disciples. Where two are touching and agreeing on a thing, it will come to pass. Husband and wife. (Matthew 18:19) We are to bring God's Kingdom into the earth through us. The children will get raised in the admonition of the Lord.

Be careful what you name your kids, speak over your kids.

They will identify with what you call them and what you say to and about them.

Jacob's favorite wife was dying as she gave birth to the 12th son and called him Benoni, which means, "son of my pain" or "son of my misfortune." Jacob changed his name to Benjamin. Benjamin means, "son of my right hand."

Jacob's name was changed by God to Israel. Jacob means "trickster, supplanter, heal grabber." Israel means "prince of God."

And Jabez was more honourable than his brethren: and his mother called his name Jabez, saying, Behold I bare him with sorrow (1 Chron 4:9-11, Jabez)

You are prophesying the future.

Declare things that are not as though they were. (Romans 4:16-22)

You cannot, dare not love your husband, your wife with your flesh. That's not Kingdom. That's the world. In this flesh is no good thing. Seek your husband, seek your wife in the Spirit and it will manifest in the natural. Choose to be his/her Aaron and Ur when necessary. Choose to war in the Spirit against every ungodly attack. Choose to speak life, love, joy, peace, strength and you will see it manifest in the natural. Choose to love him, to love her unconditionally, sacrificially, intentionally, purposefully, on purpose. This is not about your feelings. Feelings are fickle. Feelings are temporary. Pray before speaking or taking action on anything; even if it's from your husband or wife. Hug him/her. Pray for him/her. Do not respond in kind. That old saying, "Two wrongs don't make a right." Pray. Pray. Pray. Pray. Pray. Pray. I cannot say that enough. Pray. Forgive. That's a MUST. Do NOT give the enemy an opening. Do NOT give the enemy an opening. Do NOT give the enemy an opening. Repeat: I will NOT give the enemy an opening.

The Virtuous woman (Proverbs 31 wife) got up while her husband and children still slept and got before God. Ladies, you need your own prayer life. You have to go to war at times for your husband, for your children; and at times for your parents, siblings, nieces, nephews, and friends. There are times you have to go to God to keep from strangling your husband, your children and whoever else done lost their ever loving mind. Daddy! Your son, get him, Lord, before I do. Daddy! Those kids I asked for, take them before I hurt them, Lord! Lord, how about you take me home and leave them here.

God will bring together two imperfect people who will love each other as God loves us; will see each other as God sees us.

Husband,

God gave men responsibility. Men are to lead, cover, protect, and provide. We are to go where God tells us, leads us. Do not leave your wife uncovered, unprotected,

and without provision.

Lead her like Abraham to a land where God tells you to go. God blessed Abraham because of his obedience. Many nations came from Abraham, a man who was childless. His wife was barren in her womb, but God. God will allow some things to happen so He can show up and show He is God. God opened his wife's womb and she bore him a son. Abraham wasn't perfect. He made some mistakes. He tried to help God out, as we often do.

Fight for her like Jacob

Jacob worked 14 years for his wife, Rachel. This is why the bridegroom lifts the veil from the bride, so he will see, for sure, who he's marrying.

Care for her like Boaz

Boaz protected and provided for Ruth. He told the young men not to touch her. Boaz noticed Ruth while she was gleaning the fields. She was working to bring home food for her and her mother in law. Boaz heard of her reputation; how she left behind all she knew, her family and her home, a familiar place; a familiar people, familiar gods.

Love her like Christ

Jesus sacrificed His life for His Bride so that His Bride would be redeemed, made whole, have life abundantly, to prosper and be in good health as His Bride's soul prospers.

The husband is to love and sacrifice like Jesus.

Your husband, your wife is not to be placed before God. Man is not to be placed before God. Man did not create you, bless you, give you dominion. Man did not go to the cross and die for you. Your husband, your wife is not God Almighty, is not omnipotent, is not omnipresent; cannot be everywhere at the same time, all the time.

The husband is the head of the house, the Priest of the house; to be like Jesus, to lead like Jesus. When the wife takes on the name of her husband, everything the husband represents, and all that he has is hers.

The husband and wife are to be consecrated for Kingdom Covenant.

Husband and wife are to be the embodiment of Jesus and His Church in the earth. The children of that Covenant are the disciples.

Our Father and Mother in the garden were a foreshadowing of Christ Jesus and His Church. They were given dominion and were to rule side-by-side in the earth, just as Jesus and the Church will be ruling in the earth.

The Church is God's government in the earth. We are supposed to be ruling, not the world. Yet, the world has dominion in the earth. Although Jesus rose with all power in His hands, as His Bride, we have access to the power by speaking, "In the name of Jesus." Jesus is the Church's covering, just as the husband is the wife's covering.

How can we rule and reign with Jesus, if we do not know how to rule and reign together as husband and wife in the earth?

Husband and wife, when you are talking to each other, you are talking to God's son, to God's daughter. What you're doing to each other, you're doing it to God's child; both good and evil. When man and woman come into Kingdom Covenant, God essentially becomes your Father-in-love. Love is God's law. God's laws are His commandments. God does not demand us to do anything. We have free will. His love commands us to do His will.

Ladies, my dear sisters, keep your mouths off your husbands. Husbands, love your wives as Christ loves the Church.

Wives, women, how you talk to Jesus is how you're supposed to talk to your husbands.

Husbands, men, how Jesus loves the Church is how you're supposed to love your wives.

The husband carries a weight that his wife should help bear up. The wife carries a weight that her husband should help bear up.

Pray for each other. Sow into each other.

The wife brings the husband favor. *Do not mistake it to mean that your husband should be kissing your feet and doting on you like you're all that and a bag of chips. That's pride and arrogance; manipulation.* Would you treat Jesus that way? Keep your mouth off your husband unless you're speaking life and blessings into and over his life.

Your husband is your covering. Would you curse who is covering you? Would you curse Jesus?

As Apostle Paul says, there is no good thing in the flesh. He crucified the flesh daily. For I know that in me (that is, my flesh) dwelleth no good thing: for to will is present with me; but how to perform that which is good I find not. (Romans 7:18)

This I say then, Walk in the Spirit, and ye shall not fulfill the lust of the flesh. 17 For the flesh lusteth against the Spirit, and the Spirit against the flesh; and these are contrary to the other: so that ye cannot do things that we would. (Galatians 5:16-17)

Watch and pray, that ye enter not into temptation: the spirit indeed is willing, but the flesh is weak. (Matthew 26:41)

Do not leave a chink in your armour for the devil to use. (Ephesians 6:10-18)

Guard your tongue. Ask the Holy Ghost to guard your tongue. (James 3)

Pray before you speak. It's okay to be angry, but sin not. Do not let the sun set on your wrath. (Ephesians 4:26) In other words, do not hold onto your anger and let it simmer and pour out on the next day. The enemy will give you some thoughts, some suggestions on how you should handle your feelings. Do not let a temporary situation cause you to make a permanent decision. Talk to Esau.

> *Pastor Jentzen Franklin: A woman is a multiplier. When a man gives a woman his seed, she will multiply it and give him a baby. Give a woman a house and she will multiply it and make it a home. Give a woman trouble and she will multiply it, pressed down, shaken together and running over, will she give it back to you. (LOL)*

In the same way, you husbands, live with your wives in an understanding way [with great gentleness and tact, and with an intelligent regard for the marriage relationship], as with someone physically weaker, since she is a woman. Show her honor and respect as a fellow heir of the grace of life, so that your prayers will not be hindered or ineffective. (1 Peter 3:7, read 1- 8)

> *Areas that break up marriages – Dr. Jamal-Harrison Bryant*
>
> 1. *Income*
> 2. *Intimacy (frequency, quality, quantity, fidelity). The bedroom is undefiled*
> 3. *Imagination (undiscussed expectations)*

1 Corinthian 7:2-5
> 1b It is good for a man not to touch a woman
>
> 2 Nevertheless, to avoid fornication, let every man have his own wife, and let every woman have her own husband
>
> 3 Let the husband render unto the wife due benevolence; and likewise, also the wife unto the husband
>
> 4 The wife hath not power of her own body, but the husband: and likewise, also the husband hath not power of his own body, but the wife
>
> 5 Defraud ye not one the other, except it be with consent for a time, that ye may give yourselves to fasting and praying; and come together again, that Satan tempt you not for your incontinency

Marriage is honorable, and the bed undefiled: but whoremongers and adulterers God will judge (Hebrews 13:4)

Matthew 19:4b-6, 4b Have you not read, that He which made them at the beginning, made them male and female 5 And said, For this cause shall a man leave father and mother, and shall cleave to his wife; and they twain shall be one flesh? 6 Wherefore they are no more twain, but one flesh. What therefore God hath joined together, let no man put asunder.

What God hath joined together, not man.

Unless a house is built on the solid rock, the solid foundation, it will not withstand storms. (Matthew 7:24-27)

A house divided will not stand. (Matthew 12:25)

Except the Lord build the house, they labor in vain that build it; except the Lord keep the city, the watchman waketh but in vain. (Psalm 127:1)

Your wife shall be like a fruitful vine within your house; your sons, like olive saplings around your table. (Psalm 128:3, Tanakh)

God knows what we need before we ask. (Matthew 6:8)

We are to bring God's Kingdom into the earth. (Matthew 6:9-13)

Kingdom Covenant is God's will and purpose in the earth…through husband and wife.

Kingdom Covenant was and is God's plan from the beginning. The Covenant (marriage) between husband and wife is a microcosm (shadow) of Jesus and His Church. It is God who calls each of us out of sin to reign with His Son. One song says, "This is just a rehearsal."

Enjoy happiness with a woman you love all the fleeting days of life that have been granted to you under the sun—all your fleeting days. For that alone is what you can get out of life and out of the means you acquire under the sun. (Ecclesiastes 9:9, Tanakh)

Our Mother and Father were naked and unashamed before God and each other.

They weren't hiding anything, who they were. Husbands and wives should be friends, naked and unashamed in each other's presence. Husbands and wives should be able to share the deep things of their souls. Husbands and wives must first experience that with God one on one, so they can experience one on one with each other.

God knows everything, so why hide it. God will not repeat your secrets.

Husbands and wives should have that same safe space, place with each other.

God said to a nation, Come now, and let us reason together, saith the Lord (Isaiah 1:18a) Can two walk together, except they be agreed? (Amos 3:3)

There is no more condemnation in Christ Jesus, who walk not after the flesh, but after the Spirit. (Romans 8:1)

You are a new creature in Christ Jesus; old things are passed away; behold all things are new. (2 Corinthians 5:17)

Forgetting those things that are behind and reaching forward to what lies ahead (Philippians 3:13-14)

When we say God knows the end from the beginning, do we believe that for every area of our lives? Or only for certain areas? i.e., Work. Career. Illness. Finances. Valley experiences.

Chapter 5 | Husband and Wife

God's love is sacrificial, unconditional, intentional, on purpose, and purposeful.

Love is not about how you feel at any given moment to decide what you should do or be doing. Love is a decision. Love is responsibility. Love is choosing to be responsible for how you talk to, do for, treat, how you make the object, the person, feel. Regardless of how you feel, love does. Love does not hold back giving, doing. That's what the world does. Kingdom love is sacrificial, unconditional, intentional, on purpose, purposeful.

Love is a choice. Love is action. If you get, when you get tired, frustrated, emotional, or however you are feeling at that time, choose to love your husband, your wife; by still doing for him, for her. You will need to pray before you move; yet still choose to love your husband, your wife.

Prayer is the key to Heaven. Prayer is the key to peace, to joy. You will not feel it all the time; however, prayer changes attitudes, changes situations, calms anxieties, lifts burdens. While you are focused on Kingdom business, God is taking care of your business.

> *Husband and wife were debating over who was responsible for making the coffee in the morning. The husband told his wife that she's responsible because she's the woman. The wife responded and said, "The Bible says Hebrews."*

If you can be one with Jesus, then you, husband and wife, can be one with each other. The God in the husband comes together with the God in the wife. You cannot come together in your flesh. That reaps corruption. You must come together in Spirit.

We are Spirit housed in mortal flesh, having a human experience.

You are not equal with God. You can become one with God in Spirit and in Truth.

God wants to partner with you, husband and wife, in bringing His Kingdom into the earth where it once was; the garden of Eden.

God chooses us, these earthen vessels, to love another; to show His love through one another, and in one another.

Bishop Noel Jones did a demonstration at a conference. He called Dr. Juanita Bynum and a man to help him. He had them face each other and Bishop Jones played the role of God. He put his arms through the arms, rather, under the arms of the man, and reached and touched Dr. Bynum and stated, "God wants to love her through you." Then, Bishop Jones did the same thing with Dr. Bynum and said, "God wants to love him through you."

God is a Spirit. Yes, He can manifest into anyone or anything He chooses. So, He chose and chooses to manifest in and through Man. Let us make Man in our image and after our likeness. Man is to be just like God. We are God in the earth. We were created to love one another.

Kingdom Covenant is bringing God's Kingdom into the earth through the husband and wife.

Love does not abandon ship. Love keeps the ship floating.

The storms will rock and toss the ship. If you call on Jesus, speak peace be still, Jesus will get you through the storms as a couple. If you have a prayer life, Jesus is in the boat with you. The Holy Ghost that dwells in you and with you will guide you through or around the storms. If there are disciples, children, your relationship with your wife, your husband must be united, strong. Your children are your disciples.

Your family is as strong as your Covenant with each other. Action speaks louder than words. i.e., I can show you better than I can tell you. Love is action. Love does when feelings won't.

If you do not have a prayer life, you will set the course of dysfunction for generations.

God is a God of generations. He doesn't just look at (consider) you. He looks at Abraham, Isaac, and Jacob. Father, son, and grandson.

Husbands and wives, if your marriage isn't ministered to, raising children together will not be well. Wives, don't use the babies as a shield. If you're in post-partum depression, seek a counselor, preferably a Christian counselor. Husbands, do not play the guilt game, saying, "You love that baby more than you love me." Don't do it. Your wife's body and hormones have changed significantly. Give her a spa day, even if it's home; draw her a bath; light some candles, put some rose pedals and fragrant oil in the water. Love on your wife and she will love on you.

Stop demanding obedience, submission, and command it.

The way a man loves a woman is not the same as a parent loving a child. Yes, it should be unconditional, sacrificial, intentional, on purpose, purposeful. The intimacy between a man and woman is not the same.

Wife, your husband is not your son, so you do not need to train him; nor is he your pet. You are not his mother. Sisters, you are not your mother. There are ways that we inherit because we were raised under it. That does not mean you should be doing what your mother did.

Seek ye first the Kingdom of God and His righteousness; and all you need will be provided. Spouse second. Children. Work/Business/Ministry. Hobbies. Everything you do, do it unto God.

Pray for each other. Pray together…daily. Do not leave an opening for Satan.

Satan was able to get next to our Mother in the garden of Eden because she and our Father were at that tree. The temptation was already there, so all Satan had to do was make suggestions. Husbands, don't allow anyone to walk up to your wife. Cover her.

Satan knows if he could get next to your wife, he could destroy the sanctity of that Covenant. Wives, don't try to get your husbands to do what you want him to do. (Genesis 3:1-8) Husbands, don't be letting just anyone approach your wives. Guard your favor.

Satan saw another chance to reign on the throne in the garden of Eden.

Husbands and wives, don't you give Satan a chance to reign in your garden of Eden.

It starts with suggestions that will eventually have you suspecting each other; does he/she really love me? Does he flirt with other women? Does my wife have a "work husband?" Husbands, don't you allow a two-legged serpent whisper in your wife's ear, making her question who she is to you. Cover your wives. Don't allow pride and arrogance to creep in saying, "They can flirt with her because she's coming home with me." Don't get an ego - edging God out - while inviting Satan in through pride and arrogance.

Wives, I don't care what the enemy puts in your head, keep your mouth off your husband. You are to respect and honor your husband for his sacrifice. How are you to reign with Jesus if you cannot reign with hour husband? The husband is the Priest in the home. Husbands, your wife is your God-given favor, not your slave. She is your rib, not your backbone or foot bone.

Protect your garden of Eden. Wives, your husbands are your covering. Don't you offer your husband forbidden fruit. Don't be accepting messages from men. I don't care how flattering you find it. As God told Eve, "Your desire shall be for your husband only."

Husband and wife, you should be so focused on your own tree that you wouldn't have time to be lusting after someone else's tree. Tend to your own garden so that you won't even take a glimpse at your neighbor's garden.

Not everyone has the same fruit. If you've been chosen to have an apple tree; if you tend it well, God will give you an orchard. If you've been chosen to have an orange tree, tend it well, and God will give you an orange grove.

When Satan tries to plant seeds in your mind; such as, that orchard belongs to you, or that orange grove was supposed to be yours, tell that devil God did not make a mistake. I have what I am supposed to have; nothing more, nothing less.

It's not IF the devil will attack this Covenant; It's when, so pray, pray, pray. Do not search for attacks; recognize the attacks when they do come. A thief will look for an entrance no matter how secure the house looks. You have the Holy Ghost and legions of Angels as security; make sure you keep them employed (engaged). The issue, the task may seem small to you but it's not too small for God.

There's a weight that is on the husband. There's a weight that's on the wife. There will be times when the husband will carry some of the weight of his wife. There will be a time when the wife will carry some of the weight of her husband. Do not tell the other, "Suck it up." You should be saying, "Get some rest, I got you."

Intimacy – into me you see

Husbands and wives should not be wearing masks, nor feel they should with each other. A man's true rib would see beyond what everyone else sees. Because his wife is his true rib, he would see beyond what everyone else sees. They would be a reflection of each other, yet have their own individuality, yet fit perfectly together.

The wife is woman, his womb. The wife is the female, the feminine to his masculine. A womb carries, gestates. Feminine is a soft place, a vulnerability. The husband is the masculine to your feminine. He is a safe, secure place to lean on.

There's strength in a woman that makes hell nervous, demons flee.

Satan knows this and that's why he approached our Mother in the garden.

Satan knows your power better than you do. Satan knows you better than you do.

The garden of Eden was God's Kingdom in the earth. Satan recognized that. Keep in mind, Satan lived in Heaven. He was a part of God's Kingdom. The garden of Eden was another chance for him to rule and reign on God's throne.

You are a threat to Satan. Heaven is on your side. He knows that if you knew who you are and walk and live out the purpose of Kingdom Covenant, you would tear down his kingdom. ***He knows as long as we are divided, he gets to wreak havoc a little longer.*** This is why Satan has been destroying God's children. First, he knows his time is short. Second, Man has the authority to destroy his kingdom. Third, Satan truly hates Man.

We are to model to our families, the Church, the single people, the World, what God's Kingdom looks like.

Keep in mind, we are Spirit wrapped in flesh having a human experience.

What we do in the earth is all preparation to reign with Christ Jesus. How can we reign with Christ Jesus if we do not learn to reign as husband and wife?

God is commanding us to take our rightful place in the earth. He gave Man dominion from the beginning.

Wisdom and Guidance

Proverbs 5:15-23

15 Drink water from your own cistern [of a pure marriage relationship] and fresh running water from your own well. 16 Should your springs (children) be dispersed, as streams of water in the streets? 17 [Confine yourself to your own wife.] Let your children be yours alone, and not the children of strangers with you. 18 Let your fountain (wife) be blessed [with the rewards of fidelity], and rejoice in the wife of your youth. 19 Let her be as the loving hind and pleasant roe; let her breasts satisfy you at all times; and be exhilarated and delight in her love. 20 Why should you, my son, be exhilarated with an immoral woman and embrace the bosom of an outsider (pagan)? 21 For the ways of man are directly before the eyes of the Lord, and he carefully watches all of his paths [all of his comings and goings]. 22 The iniquities done by a wicked man will trap him, and he will be held with the cords of this sin. 23 He will die for lack of instruction (discipline); and in the greatness of his foolishness, he will go astray.

A wise man leaves an inheritance for his children's children. (Proverbs 13:22)

Proverbs (AMP)
    12:4 A virtuous woman and excellent wife [worthy of honor] is a crown to her husband; but she that shames him [with her foolishness] is like rottenness in his bones

    19:14 Houses and riches are the inheritance from fathers, but a wise, understanding and sensible wife is [a gift and blessing] from the Lord

Chapter 5 | Husband and Wife

Proverbs 6:20-25 (AMP)

20 My son, be guided by your father's [God-given] commandment (instruction) and do not reject the teaching of your mother. 21 Bind them continually upon your heart (in your thoughts), and tie them around your neck. 22 When you walk about, they (the godly teachings of your parents) will guide you; when you sleep, they will keep watch over you; and when you awake, they will talk to you. 23 For the commandment is a lamp, and the teaching [of the law] is light, and reproofs (rebukes) for discipline are the way of life. 24 To keep you from the evil woman, from [the flattery of] the smooth tongue of an immoral woman. 25 Do not desire (lust after) her beauty in your heart, nor let her capture you with her eyelashes.

Proverbs 7:1-5 1 My son, keep my words, and treasure my commandments within you [so they are readily available to guide you]. 2 Keep my commandments and live; and keep my teaching and law as the apple of your eye. 3 Bind them [securely] on your fingers, write them upon the tablet of your heart. 4 Say to [skillful and godly] wisdom, "You are my sister," and regard understanding and intelligent insight as your intimate friends; 5 That they may keep you from the immoral woman, from the foreigner [who does not observe God's law and] who flatters with her [smooth] words.

An unruly wife/woman is like...

Proverbs 19:13-14 (AMP)

A foolish (ungodly) son is destruction to his father, and the contentions of a [quarrelsome] wife are like a constant dripping [of water]. 14 House and wealth are the inheritance from fathers, but a wise, understanding, and sensible wife is [a gift and blessing] from the Lord.

Proverbs 27:15 (AMP)

A constant dripping on a day of steady rain and a contentious (quarrelsome) woman are alike

A gracious wife/woman is like (read Proverbs 11)

Proverbs 11:16 (AMP)

A gracious and good woman attains honor, and ruthless men attain riches [but not respect]

Proverbs 14:1 (AMP)

The wise woman builds her house [on a foundation of godly precepts, and her household thrives], but the foolish one [who lacks spiritual insight] tears it down with her own hands [by ignoring godly principles.

Ecclesiastes 9:9 (Tanakh)

Enjoy happiness with a woman you love all the fleeting days of life that have been granted to you under the sun-all your fleeting days. For that alone is what you can get out of life and out of the means you acquire under the sun.

Live joyfully with the wife whom thou loveth all the days of the life of thy vanity, which he hath given thee under the sun, all the days of thy vanity: for that is thy portion in this life, and in thy labour which thou takest under the sun (KJV)

You are supposed to be living, breathing, walking, talking tabernacles of the Holy Ghost.

PRAYERS

You cannot pour out of an empty carton, glass, soul. You're human. Recognize it. Embrace it. Stay connected to the source, God's Kingdom. Do not feel guilty for saying, "No."

Speak things that are not as though they were over your spouse, your children, your family, your ministry; Death and life are in the power of the tongue; and they that love it shall eat the fruit thereof. (Proverbs 18:21)

How can you go to war with an enemy that knows you better than you know you? You do tell the enemy all your business by what you say and what you do.

Be strategic in prayer; don't babble. Speak the Word of God. You cannot speak it if you don't know it. Read your bible. It's living. It's the Bread of Heaven. It's Living Water. Declare, Lord, feed me till I want no more; quench this thirsting in my soul.

Satan is here to steal, kill, and destroy by whatever means necessary.

Walk daily with the person of the Holy Ghost.

Why marriages fail is that God is not invited to be a part of the Covenant.

Husband, speak to God's daughter, your wife, the mother of your children, businesswoman, entrepreneur, sister, friend.

Wife, speak to God's son, your husband, the father of your children, businessman, entrepreneur, brother friend.

You are fearfully and wonderfully made in the image and after the likeness of God. You are His masterpiece. You are more than a conqueror through Christ Jesus. Greater is He that is in you than he that is in the world. You are powerful. You are the daughter or son of the Almighty God

Song of Solomon
> 1:2 Oh, give me the kisses of your mouth, for your love is more delightful than wine; 10 Your cheeks are comely with plaited wreaths, your neck with strings of jewels; 13 My beloved to me is a spray of henna blooms from the vineyards of Engedi; 16 And you, my beloved, are handsome, beautiful indeed!
>
> 2:5 Sustain me with raisin cakes, refresh me with apples, for I am faint with love; 6 His left hand was under my head, his right arm embraced me
>
> 5:14 His hands are rods of gold, studded with beryl; his belly a tablet of ivory, adorned with sapphires; 15 His legs are like marble pillars set in sockets of fine gold. He is majestic as Lebanon, stately as the cedars; 16 His mouth is delightful. Such is my beloved, such is my darling, O maidens of Jerusalem!

You are a wise mother or father. You are equipped for this. You will raise up your children in the fear and admonition of the Lord. They are the fruit of your womb and your loins, so they will do very well. They are brilliant. God trusted us with His creation.

You are a virtuous woman. You are a powerful and resilient man. You are admired. Your hands are blessed, fruitful. God blessed you with gifts to be fruitful, to multiply and fill the earth with.

Proverbs 31

Chapter 6

Chapter 6 | Proverbs 31

The Chayil or Virtuous Woman is a woman of God walking in and living out her God-given purpose

KJV 10 Who can find a virtuous woman? For her price is far above rubies

AMP 10 An excellent woman [one who is spiritual, capable, intelligent, and virtuous], who is he who can find her? Her value is more precious than jewels and her worth is far above rubies or pearls [Prov 12:4; 18:22; 19:14]

Tanakh 10 What a rare find is a capable wife! Her worth is far beyond that of rubies.

This woman is strong in the Lord. She is able to do what she has been called to do. She has high moral standards, righteous and principled.

KJV 11 The heart of her husband doth safely trust in her, so that he shall have no need of spoil

AMP 11 The heart of her husband trust in her [with secure confidence], and he will have no lack of gain

Tanakh 11 Her husband puts his confidence in her, and lacks no good thing

This woman's husband has no worries and is anxious for nothing.

KJV 12 She will do him good and not evil all the days of her life

AMP 12 She comforts, encourages, and does him only good and not evil all the days of her life

Tanakh 12 She is good to him, never bad, all the days of her life

This is the heart and the will of a virtuous woman. Due to her virtue, she loves, honors and respects her husband.

KJV 13 She seeketh wool, and flax, and worketh willingly with her hands

AMP 13 She looks for wool and flax and works with willing hands in delight

Tanakh 13 She looks for wool and flax, and sets her hand to them with a will

This woman pursues, searches for the merchandise she needs for her business.

KJV 14 She is like the merchant ships; she bringeth her food from afar

AMP 14 She is like the merchant ships [abounding with treasure]; she brings her [household's] food from far away

Tanakh 14 She is like a merchant fleet, bringing her food from afar

This woman purchases the best of the best food for her household. Keep in mind there weren't freezers and refrigerators 3,000 years ago. Therefore, the food was fresh and healthy.

KJV 15 She riseth also while it is yet night, and giveth meat to her household, and a portion to her maidens

AMP 15 She rises also while it is still night and gives food to her household and assigns tasks to her maids [Job 23:12]

Tanakh 15 She rises while it is still night, and supplies provisions for her household, the daily fare of her maids

This woman plans and prepares for the day ahead. Lord, give us this day, our daily bread.

KJV 16 She considereth a field, and buyeth it: with the fruit of her hands she planteth a vineyard

AMP 16 She considers a field before she buys or accepts it [expanding her business prudently]; with her profits she plants fruitful vines in her vineyard

Tanakh 16 She sets her mind on an estate and acquires it; she plants a vineyard by her own labors

This woman does her due diligence (homework) before purchasing land. Then plants a vineyard, which will create another stream of income.

KJV 17 She girdeth her loins with strength, and stengtheneth her arms

AMP 17 She equips herself with strength [spiritual, mental, and physical fitness for her God-given task] and makes her arms strong

Tanakh 17 She girds herself with strength, and performs her tasks with vigor

This woman girds herself with truth (Ephesians 6:14) and God-given strength to perform her tasks with vitality and physical strength.

KJV 18 She perceiveth that her merchandise is good: her candle goeth not out by night

AMP 18 She sees that her gain is good; her lamp does not go out, but it burns continually through the night [she is prepared for whatever lies ahead]

Tanakh 18 She sees that her business thrives; her lamp never goes out at night

This woman recognizes, discerns that her merchandise is good because of how she works, the materials she uses; she is not lazy in her tasks.

KJV 19 She layeth her hands to the spindle, and her hands hold the distaff

AMP 19 She stretches out her hands to the distaff, and her hands hold the spindle [as she spins wool into thread for clothing]

Tanakh 19 She sets her hand to the distaff; her finders work the spindle

This woman prepares wool, flax and silk to make clothing for her household and business.

KJV 20 She stretcheth out her hand to the poor; yea, she reacheth forth her hands to the needy

AMP 20 She opens and extends her hand to the poor, and she reaches out her filled hands to the needy

Tanakh 20 She gives generously to the poor; her hands are stretched out to the needy

He who is generous to the poor make a loan to the Lord; He will repay him his due. (Proverbs 19:17 Tanakh)

For I was hungry, and you gave Me something to eat; I was thirsty; and you gave Me something to drink; I was a stranger, and you invited Me in; I was naked and you clothed Me..(Matthew 25:35-36)

This woman is blessed because of her generosity. She shall reap a bountiful harvest; multiple streams of income shall be her portion.

KJV 21 She is not afraid of the snow for her household; for all her household are clothed with scarlet

AMP 21 She does not fear the snow for her household, for all in her household are clothed in [expensive] scarlet [wool].

Tanakh 21 She is not worried for her household because of snow. For her whole household is dressed in crimson

The Virtuous Woman's prayer keeps her household covered with the Blood of Jesus. Her household is covered both physically and spiritually.

KJV 22 She maketh herself coverings of tapestry; her clothing is silk and purple

AMP 22 She makes for herself coverlets, cushions, and rugs of tapestry. Her clothing is linen, pure and fine, and purple [wool]

Tanakh 22 She makes covers for herself; her clothing is linen and purple

This woman clothes her household with clothing, makes household goods fit for royalty.

KJV 23 Her husband is known in the gates, when he sitteth among the elders of the land

AMP 23 Her husband is known in the [city's] gates, when he sits among the elders of the land [Prov 12:4]

Tanakh 23 Her husband is prominent in the gates, as he sits among the elders of the land

This woman's virtue causes her husband to be respected of the elders who sit at the city gates; her husband is recognized by the people coming in and going out.

KJV 24 She maketh fine linen, and selleth it; and delivereth girdles unto the merchant

AMP 24 She makes [fine] linen garments and sells them; and supplies sashes to the merchants

Tanakh 24 She makes cloth and sells it, and offers a girdle to the merchant

This woman sells fine clothing and is blessed to give girdles to the merchants where she sells her goods.

KJV 25 Strength and honour are her clothing; and she shall rejoice in time to come

AMP 25 Strength and dignity are her clothing and her position is strong and secure; and she smiles at the future [knowing that she and her family are prepared]

Tanakh 25 She is clothed with strength and splendor; she looks to the future cheerfully

This woman is clothed with strength, honor, dignity and she wears it well. Her household is without worry because of this woman.

KJV 26 She openeth her mouth with wisdom; and in her tongue is the law of kindness

AMP 26 She opens her mouth in [skillful and godly] wisdom, and the teaching of kindness is on her tongue [giving counsel and instruction]

Tanakh 26 Her mouth is full of wisdom; her tongue with kindly teaching

This woman speaks with godly knowledge and wisdom. She guides and teaches with wise and kind counsel.

KJV 27 She looketh well to the ways of her household, and eateth not the bread of idleness

AMP 27 She looks well to how things go in her household, and does not eat the bread of idleness

Tanakh 27 She oversees the activities of her household and never eats the bread of idleness

This woman sees that her household lacks nothing. She is not lazy.

KJV 28 Her children rise up, and call her blessed; her husband also, and he praiseth her

AMP 28 Her children rise up and call her blessed (happy, prosperous, to be admired); her husband also, and he praises her saying,

Tanakh 28 Her children declare her happy; her husband praises her

KJV 29 Many daughters have done virtuously, but thou excellest them all

AMP 29 Many daughters have done nobly, and well [with the strength and character that is steadfast in goodness], but you excel them all

Tanakh 29 Many women have done well, but you surpass them all

This woman takes very good care of her husband and children. She is up early yet does not go to sleep until she prepares for the next day. Her household lacks nothing. She seeks the Lord early before she sets out to do anything.

KJV 30 Favour is deceitful, and beauty is vain: but a woman that feareth the Lord, she shall be praised;

AMP 30 Charm and grace are deceptive, and [superficial] beauty is vain, but a woman who fears the Lord [reverently worshiping, obeying, serving, and trusting Him with awe-filled respect], she shall be praised;

Tanakh 30 Grace is deceptive, beauty is illusory; it is for her fear of the Lord that a woman is to be praised;

KJV 31 Give her of the fruit of her hands; and let her own works praise her in the gates.

AMP 31 Give her of the product of her hands, and let her own works praise her in the gates [of the city]

Tanakh 31 Extol her for the fruit of her hand, and let her works praise her in the gates

This virtuous woman has a spirit of excellence because she prays and trusts the Lord to bless the works of her hands. Therefore, she will not lack any good thing. The Lord will give her the desires of her heart and bless the plans she laid out for her multiple businesses. A virtuous woman is mighty in the Lord. This virtuous woman is submitted to and covered by her godly, righteous husband.

V10 cr Ruth 3:11; Proverbs 12:4; 19:14

V15 cr Proverbs 20:13; Romans 12:11; Luke 12:42

V20 Deuteronomy 15:11; Job 31:16-20; Proverbs 22:9; Romans 12:13; Ephesians 4:28; Hebrews 13:16

V21 [Joshua 2:18,19; Heb 9:19-22]

V22 [Isaiah 61:10; 1 Timothy 2:9; Revelations 3:5; 19:8, 14]

V23 Proverbs 12:4

V27 [1 Timothy 5:14; Titus 2:5]

V32 [Phil 4:8]

Consecrate For Covenant

We Consecrate for Ministry. Why not for Marriage?
Is Marriage not a Ministry?

Chapter 7

Wife

Prepare like Esther
Honor like Ruth
Pray as bold as Hannah
Go to war like Deborah
Expect the impossible like Sarai
Sit at Jesus' feet like Mary

Husband

Learn to lead like Abraham
Cover like Boaz
Love like Jesus
Fight for her like Jacob
Speak to her like Solomon in Songs of Solomon

Consecration....

- Surrender – submit your will to Jesus' will
- Read the Word (Bible)
- Pray without ceasing
- Declare and decree the Word
- Renounce old ways of thinking, doing, living
- Get intimate with Jesus – tell him even your deepest secrets. They will never be repeated. The more you spend time in prayer, reading the Word, decreeing and declaring, the more intimate and free you'll become. Nake and unashamed.

This journey of consecration hasn't been easy. It truly has been a faith walk; a spiritual awakening; a lot of growth; and learning to grow through and not just go through. The lessons are invaluable. An Ivy League education cannot compare.

God is the center of my life. He is supposed to be. The world we are born into is a fallen and sinful world. That's why we must be born again

Now, I can boldly declare….

Oh, how You walk with me

Oh, how You talk with me

Oh, how You tell me that I am Your own

I walk and talk daily with the person of the Holy Ghost. I Pray. I read the Bible. I declare and decree God's Word. I meditate on His Word. As I did that, God changed me.

Everything Jesus is, I am. I take on Jesus' identity the more I spend time with Him and become one with Him. Bridegroom and Bride. I am to be bone of His bones, flesh of His flesh. I am Christian. I am who He says I am. Jesus' side was pierced for me.

Light follows light.

I stand before God, in the name of Jesus Christ, naked and unashamed. I am His masterpiece. I am wonderfully and fearfully made in His image and after His likeness. He gave me dominion in the earth. Jesus said greater things will I do.

I can say that now….

My life prior….

I did not have a prayer life. I would talk to God every once in a while. God, I don't want to date anyone. I needed to work on me, my self-esteem; yet, not realizing what I was saying was spiritual and not natural. I kept meeting the same kind of man, just a different name and different look; selfish, self-centered. I heard, "You attract who you are, so I had to ask myself was I that way? The answer was no, so why was I attracting that kind of man? Did I have "sucker" or "gullible" written on my face? Or across my forehead?

I was listening to the advice of people instead of the One who made us when it came to personal relationships. I wouldn't date for years at a time. It would be the same thing all over again. I wanted to settle down and get married; however, more prepared and wiser with my choice. I was still in the world listening to worldly advice.

I dated the same man that I had married after the divorce, a few times. I had an unwritten list of who I wanted and God gave me exactly who was on that unwritten list. (I had verbally expressed what kind of man I wanted to God.) Same man with a different name. The last man I was in a relationship with, God used to draw me closer to Himself than I had ever been for the entirety of my life up to that point. I did not know God, so I did not know myself. I said I knew my worth and would not settle, but I really did not. Because I did not know God; therefore, I did not know who and whose I am. Once I got in the Word of God, the Word of God changed me. I declared over and over I will not accept anyone nor anything less than God's best for me. God taught me about me by teaching me about Him.

I was married to someone who was supposed to have been a Believer, but he didn't take me to Church. I don't recall him going while we were married. He didn't pray for me and I didn't pray for him. His Mom invited me to Church when my daughters were toddlers. The experience was not good. The people in front of me talked the whole time. I cannot even tell you what the Preacher said.

I was raised by two people that got saved together when I was a young child; however, they did not become whole, healed individuals. They argued and fought occasionally. I remember them going to special evening Church services. However, their relationship with each other did not change.

I refused to be my parents. I refused to live their lives and my future children to live in an abusive household. Yet, I ended up marrying a man that was abusive. I did not stay there. I had two small children and refused to live that way and have them grow up the same way I did. I took a year to decide whether I wanted a divorce or could it work out. Well, I filed for divorce after 6 years of marriage.

I was in love with the idea of marriage and not truly understanding marriage.

I visited God's houses as a child and young adult. I said yes to Jesus at 20 years old, and did not remember until the Holy Ghost reminded me many years later. Today, I can tell you where I was and what I was doing when Jesus came to me in a vision.

I was more focused on what I was not going to accept based on my parents' relationship; yet did not know what I should be accepting or expecting. I was still searching for who I was, while married, while raising kids, while attaining a higher education, while working. It was not until I truly met Jesus that I became (and still am becoming) who God called me to be. It's on-going. It's daily.

The journey....

Even after coming out of the world and joining a Church, I still had a lot to learn. I still had my unwritten list of the husband I wanted, down to the physical description. Well, God put that man in my path. He's in ministry. He was my Ishmael. He looked like the promise, but was not. I did not have a prayer life before meeting him. Listen, I talked to God EVERY DAY; in the shower, in my car, on the job, every chance I had. I started watching Christian networks and reading God's Word. I was never the one to settle; however, once I understood and came into the knowledge of who and whose I am, no two-legged serpent can tell me otherwise. I could look back on my life and see God's hand moving people, places, and things from my life. I thought I was in love. I didn't have a clue of what or who love was. Now that I know what I know, I will never accept anything nor anyone less than God's best for me. I will not accept what the enemy calls me or says about what I am or who I am or where I can go. I am a child of the God Almighty. I am royalty. I am His king in the earth. I am His Lord in the earth. I am His son. I am of the Tribe of Judah. I am the Bride of Christ Jesus. I am His government in the earth. I am His Prophet. I am His intercessor. I am His Evangelist. I am called and equipped for such a time as this. I will speak to the nations. I am a soldier in the army of the Lord.

Before that....

I had to completely surrender my will, everything that I was to become who I am right now. I am still in the process of becoming. Faith to Faith. Glory to Glory. Until God calls me home, I am and will always be becoming. My walk changed. My talk changed. My sight changed. My perspective changed. My *in*sight changed. God changed me from the inside out. I could look back and see God's hands on me. It's like that old saying, "You can't see the forest for the trees because all you see are trees." Once God brings you out of that wilderness, you can see the forest and can see that each tree represents something in your life; people, places, things, relationships.

Ladies and Gentlemen, you need your own prayer life. You have to go to war at times for your husband, your wife, your children, and at times, for your parents, siblings, nieces, nephews, friends.

I retired April 1, 2021, a year after the world was shut down. I was working from home and would go into the office when necessary. So, that year helped me transition into retirement. My former supervisor asked me what I was going to do. I said I was going to work for God's government full time. I worked 31+ years in man's government. Now, I'll be working for my Dad's government. As I was shredding personnel documents; promotions, and probation over the course of the years, I looked back at the trials, tribulations, and the favor God gave me. I cried. I saw God's hand in all of it. I tried to leave that job, and interviewed a couple of times, to no avail. As I was looking back, and thinking about the trials and tribulations, I also saw the favor God gave me. It was in raises; yes, I got promotions as well over time; I was given favor to have a flexible work schedule. I got divorced about 5 ½ years into the job. I had the benefits such as, medical, vacation time, sick time, and personal time. More than likely, I would not have had the favor and fringe benefits needed at another job. I was divorced with two children and I had gone back to school. So, during that time, I grew up while raising two children and attained a Bachelor's degree. Those 31+ years was a Bachelor's, Master's, and Doctorate in different aspects of my life. The education I got is priceless. I was a civil servant. I worked with people from all walks of life. I met people from all walks of life. There are things that college does not teach you that you will learn on the job.

Everything that I had been through, matured through, grew through, especially in faith, in learning who God is, has not been wasted, not one second.

When the scripture says, "All things work together for those who love God, seek God," I can testify that it does. God kept me working for the government for 31 years to stretch me, to prepare me, to serve in adversity, at times, and in joy. I didn't like the adversity. Who does? Iron sharpens iron. I didn't have a prayer life the entire 31 years. I would talk to God every once in a while.

Today, every second I have I talk to God. I live through God. I move through God. In Him I live, in Him I move; in Him I have my very being.

The last relationship I was in God used it to do a work in me.; that at first looked like it would lead to marriage, gave me a prayer life. Look, I talked to God in the shower, in my car, everywhere. God put him on my path to teach me some things, and more importantly, to draw me closer to Him. I became a Christian. Can I take this a little deeper? I learned who and whose I was, and that changed everything, my whole perspective on that relationship and why it had to happen. God gave me exactly who I asked for to show me that's not what I wanted. I gave God a physical description. Although, I said the man had to be chasing God, BUT I didn't say he had to be my husband. There's a huge difference. You can be chasing God, yet not allowing God to change you. He and I discussed marriage and why we would marry. I sowed into someone that did not sow into me. The only time we prayed together was for travelling mercies, and over a meal. He was twice married and twice divorced.

Once I realized I was back in that familiar place of a dead-end relationship, I completely surrendered my will to God. I forgave a lot during the process. I was hurt. I was disappointed. Once I ate of the Bread of Heaven and drank from the Living Water, I lost the taste for worldly advice, opinions. I was the Samaritan woman who Jesus met at Jacob's well.

After I declared that he cannot be my husband, God released me. I mourned. I hurt. It was 4 ½ years invested in a man that wasn't my husband. At the same time, it was 4 ½ years invested in my spiritual growth, maturity. I did not regret what I grew through. If I had not learned what I did and grow through what I went through, I would have met someone just like him with a different name. He was just like the man prior, just a different name. They weren't exactly the same, just the same test that got harder. They were both sent to teach me some things about me and to show me I really didn't want what I asked for in a husband. They were both a foreshadowing of what was to come. The latter was my Ishmael.

When I look back, I could see that God was chasing after me for years to come out of the dark. When I surrendered completely to God, once I was back in that too familiar place, I asked God, "What is in me that needs to change, so that I will not continue to choose the same man again? I don't want to be back in this place again. I refuse to be back here again. Change in me what needs to change."

We say God looks at the heart of Man. The changes were not easy. I cried many tears. I'd forgiven probably every other day, many times for the same transgression. I didn't blame him. We were in different places, but both of us were in need of a heart change.

I got to a place where I could be in his presence and not feel heartache; where I could have a phone conversation and not look for a phone call or want him to call. That is because of forgiveness; that is because of Spiritual growth; that is because of truly knowing who and whose I am.

The choices I made before I got to that place in God I wouldn't make today. No.

Once you truly know who and whose you are, your choices change; what and who you listen to, watch will change; your walk will change, your talk will change; your vision will change, your perspective will change; all things become new because you are a new creation in Christ Jesus. (2 Corinthians 5:17) You become more and more like Christ.

I was on YouTube and saw a sermon by Dr. Juanita Bynum titled, "No More Sheets." It was from 1999 and I watched it in 2017. I had to divorce those men, so I followed the instructions Dr. Bynum gave; I prayed the prayer and decreed. It was a physical purging and a spiritual purging. What I mean by physical, it was like a huge amount of phlegm or mucous came up out of me. I had to run to a garbage can.

Meditating on God's Word, prayer, hearing Gods Word, listening to God's Word, building faith in God's Word, will strengthen you, will embolden you to declare everything God has spoken and has shown you will come to pass. Keep in mind, God will not send you into an unprepared place.

God planted a seed…

God planted a seed in me I was not aware of in 2015 when I attended a leadership conference in Orlando, Florida. It was my very first conference for Pastors and Leaders. I knew I had to be there. It was a birthday gift to myself; to sow into me so I may sow into others. I would end up choosing a session that my future father-in-love would teach. I don't remember the subject matter. I had not heard of him before that conference. During the Q&A, someone asked him about his son. His name didn't stick with me. It was my future father-in-love's answer that stuck with me all these years. Over the next four years, God would water, fertilize, and dig around that seed He planted.

The Lord had me praying for the man who He would reveal to me that he's my husband, I kept hearing, "I'm sending you south," I first thought it was because

I was going to sit under him as my pastor because of the "call" on my life. Then the prayers and intercession started getting personal, intimate. That's when I asked God, "Who is this man to me?" Prior to that, I was looking for a house to buy. I was thinking I would take a leave of absence from my job. When God answered my question, "Who is this man to me?" through scripture, everything changed. Instead of a leave of absence, I made plans for (early) retirement. I was surprised as to who he was/is, to say the least. Then, I asked God was I ready to be his wife; am I ready for that level? Am I enough for this man? Am I ready for this? God said, No. It didn't do much for my confidence; however, I appreciated the honesty. No, I wasn't enough, nor ready. I said, "Father, prepare me to be his wife; prepare me for this. In the Spirit, I am bold; yet, in the flesh, Lord, are you sure? Are you talking to me? Lord!"

When God showed me who my husband is, God showed me when He planted the seed and over the course of the years, He watered, fertilized, trimmed back, added more fertilizer and kept watering. I got in agreement with God's plan. It has been an emotional roller coaster, to say the least. God had my husband speak to me about himself through his testimonies, sermons, and teachings. I had my momentary doubts. I had moments where I said, "I wasn't going anywhere."

God chose my husband and I agreed with God's choice. I was bold in the Spirit and a bit intimidated in the natural. Over the course of the last few years, as I got stronger in who I am and whose I am, what would trigger emotions no longer did. "But they that wait upon the Lord shall renew their strength; they shall mount up on wings as eagles; they shall run and not get weary; shall walk and not faint. (Isaiah 40:31)

In 2015, I was not ready. The Lord had to prepare me to become his wife. His wife, not everyone or anyone else's wife. His wife. This has been *now* a nine (9) year journey. Nine years ago, I was not the woman you see today. Blessings follow obedience. It wasn't easy, yet it was worth the journey. In this journey, I had the privilege and honor to watch, follow, and learn of him.

The spiritual warfare is in another level. Witches, warlocks, sorcerers, soothsayers will attack. Your prayer, intercession has to be on that level. You need to be able to discern the spirits. There's no taking a break from warfare. You have to be able to tell those demons you cannot have my husband, my wife, my children, grandchildren. Yes, this means war. I'll go to hell and snatch them out. You have to have an "I wish you would, I dare you, you don't know who you're messing with, I'm not the one, leap over here if you want" spiritual warfare.

When my Dad took a rib from my husband to create me, then prepare me to be presented to my husband, I have been given the Grace to be his rib, his wife. I don't have the Grace to be anyone else's wife. Dad had to make sure I understood what a wife is according to Kingdom Covenant, Kingdom Principles. First, I had to understand who I am, whose I am (identity), why I am here, what's the purpose of my life, what I am supposed to be doing with what God put in me (my purpose); do I know what love is? do I know who love is? God. God's love is sacrificial, unconditional, intentional, on purpose, and purposeful. Love is not about how I feel at any given moment to decide what I should do or be doing. **Love is action.** Love is a decision. Love is responsibility. Love is choosing to be responsible for how I talk to, do for, treat, and make my husband feel. Regardless of how I feel, love does. Love does not hold back giving, doing. That's what the world does.

 If I get, when I get tired, frustrated, emotional, or however I am feeling at that time, I will choose to love my husband by still doing for him. I may need to pray before I move; yet I will still choose to love my husband. Prayer is the key to Heaven. Prayer is the key to peace, to joy. I may not feel it all the time; however, prayer changes attitudes, changes situations, calms anxieties, lifts burdens. While I am focused on Kingdom business, so to speak, God is taking care of my business.

God had me boldly declaring things in the Spirit that will eventually manifest in the earth, in the natural. Everyone and everything must come in alignment with God's plans. If I go too soon, I will mess it up because it's my flesh trying to make it happen and not God.

Although I would get anxious, God how long? I had to see and understand that my husband had to be ready to receive me. God showed me that my husband has to get to that place where he is ready to receive his wife that God has been preparing for him. That was a question I had for God. God, does he know I exist? Does he know you are preparing and have been preparing a wife for him?

God will align you with the husband or wife that would be called, chosen, and graced for that Covenant. You would decree and declare: I am called. I am chosen. I am graced to be his wife; to be her husband.

God will not leave you ignorant. If you choose not to listen, not to watch and pray, that's on you, not God.

Bishop Noel Jones did a demonstration at a conference. He called Dr. Juanita Bynum and a man to help him. He had them face each other and Bishop Jones played the role of God. He put his arms through the arms, rather under the arms of the man, and reached and touched Dr. Bynum and stated, "God wants to love her through you." Then, Bishop Jones did the same thing with Dr. Bynum and said, "God wants to love him through you."

God is Spirit. He can manifest into anyone or anything He chooses. He chooses to manifest in and through Man. Let us make Man in our image and after our likeness. Man is to be just like God. We are God in the earth. We were created to love one another.

1 Corinthians 2:9, eyes have not seen, ears have not heard, nor have hearts received the things God has for those who love Him.

My ways are not your ways; my thoughts are not your thoughts; as high as the Heaven is from the earth, are My thoughts from your thoughts, My ways from your ways. (Isaiah 55:8-9 v.10-11) God does exceedingly and abundantly above all that you can ask, think or imagine. (Ephesians 3:20)

During this preparation, I have been approached by many men via social media. Some claiming to be my husband; one insisted that he was. I thought it was rude to ignore them because of the call on my life. I specifically put a photo of me wearing a collar and that did nothing to deter. To some, it attracted them because they said they were looking for a God-fearing wife. I responded that they probably couldn't handle the calling on my life. You would have to be equipped for that and not everyone is equipped. I cannot marry just anyone. They're good looking men. Yes, there is a God in Heaven. However, they are not for me. God bless them. You have to be called, chosen, graced.

Learning from marriages...

God had me witness wives lay their husbands to rest; listen to them share their hearts and to pray for their peace. God had me witness husbands care for their dying wives and pray for their strength; cover them in prayer and speak to them, minister. God had me witness a heart-broken husband die a year after his wife. He loved his wife unconditionally, sacrificially and intentionally. She testified how her husband took care of her. I witnessed him teasing her and she would tell him to stop then giggle. This would have been 45 years of marriage (June 2024).

I do not discount or de-value the marriage vows that man wrote; the part that says, "in sickness and health, for richer or poorer, till death us do part." After being a witness to several people I knew who stood by their husbands and wives during their sickness unto death. I saw, "in sickness and in health" exemplified.

As Kingdom Citizens, we should not be experiencing sickness nor poverty nor any other care of this world; however, we live in a fallen, sinful world. This is where faith must be a way of life. You will get battle weary. I can testify to that.

I asked God, "Is this part of my ministry? Am I being selfish? Lord, what do I need to get out of this? What are you showing me?"

We grieve on many levels for many reasons. The grief of a husband, a wife, one's life partner, lover, friend, hope of the future, memories over the years, fruit in the earth.

After a divorce, there's a grieving process. After the end of a long-term relationship that did not end in marriage, but ended, there's a grieving process. You grieve what you thought it was and could've, would've, should've been. That's regret. Have a funeral and bury that regret. Grieve well. Learn and grow through the grieving process.

We say God knows the end from the beginning; that He is Alpha and Omega. Do we believe that in every area of our lives? We cannot even see around the corner, let alone days, weeks, years down the road of life. We quote Jeremiah 29:11 (and don't read v 12), but do we believe that for every area of our lives? Money is the least. The Kingdom of God is the greatest.

Do we trust God for our husbands? Our wives? He knows me, knows you; he knows the end from the beginning. Will you trust God to choose your spouse? Will you trust God to prepare you for your spouse?

When the man and woman come together before God to be joined together, that man should be a husband and that woman should be a wife. The husband should recognize his wife as bone of his bones, flesh of his flesh.

The principles for Kingdom Covenant are the same for Jesus and the Church, and for husbands and wives. The Covenant between husbands and wives are a microcosm of Jesus and His Church. How can we reign with Christ without first learning to reign in the earth as husbands and wives?

We are to bring God's Kingdom into the earth through us. The children will get raised in the admonition of the Lord. The dishes will get done. The garbage will be taken out. The bills will get paid. The everyday things will be taken care of if we seek the Kingdom of God and His righteousness first.

When Satan sees marriage, especially a true Kingdom Covenant, he will find a way, just as he did in the garden. He found a serpent willing to be used. Now he uses two-legged serpents, Man.

This is all about Genesis 1:26. God giving man dominion in the earth. Satan wanted to reign in Heaven then saw an opportunity with the garden of Eden, which was Heaven in the earth. God's Kingdom in the earth. Then Satan found an ally in a serpent.

We are to model to our families, the Church, the single people, the World, what God's Kingdom looks like.

After you say, "I do," are you taking God with you? Or are you leaving God at the altar? Was God invited?

Chapter 7 | Consecrate For Covenant

While in Consecration.....

Ladies

Prepare like Esther

Rub oils into your skin, get your hair done, or do it yourself, get your mani and pedi. Don't go out in public looking like you're about to clean your home. Esther wasn't introduced to the king until after she was prepared. Oils and perfumes were applied, of course, after being bathed. There were probably oils in the bath water. Men are carnal creatures. We first glean with our natural eyes. Adam and Eve were naked and unashamed together.

Honor like Ruth

Wherever you go, I will go. Your people shall be my people. Your God shall be my God. Where you die, I shall die. Boaz noticed Ruth while she was gleaning the fields. She was working to bring home food for her and her mother in law. Boaz heard of her reputation; how she left behind all she knew, her family and her home, a familiar place; a familiar people, familiar gods.

Pray as bold as Hannah

What Hannah sacrificed to God, God gave back to her five times. God accepted her sacrifice and blessed her. Pray bold and be willing to sacrifice.

Gentleman

God gave men responsibility. Men are to lead, cover, protect, and provide. We are to go where God tells us, leads us. Do not leave your wife uncovered, unprotected, and without provision.

Lead her like Abraham to a land where God tells you to go. God blessed Abraham because of his obedience. Many nations came from Abraham, a man who was childless. His wife was barren in her womb, but God. God will allow some things to happen so He can show up and show He is God. God opened his wife's womb and she bore him a son. Abraham wasn't perfect. He made some mistakes. He tried to help God out, as we often do.

Fight for her like Jacob

Jacob worked 14 years for his wife Rachel. This is why the bridegroom lifts the veil from the bride, so he will see for sure who he's marrying.

Care for her like Boaz

Boaz protected and provided for Ruth. He told the young men not to touch her. Boaz noticed Ruth while she was gleaning the fields. She was working to bring home food for her and her mother in law. Boaz heard of her reputation; how she left behind all she knew, her family and her home, a familiar place; a familiar people, familiar gods.

Love her like Christ

Jesus sacrificed His life for His Bride so that His Bride would be redeemed, made whole, have life abundantly, to prosper and be in good health as His Bride's soul prospers.

Healed and whole….

If you are **not** truly born again, you shouldn't even be looking to get married. The old you will absolutely wreck the marriage.

2 Corinthians 4:2 What are you renouncing? Have you decided that you will start your marriage with a clean slate, so to speak? Have you ejected, rejected past hurts, pain, disappointments, relationship gone wrong because they weren't supposed to be, hurt, rejection, unforgiveness, bitterness, uncleanness? What are you bringing with you that you should not?

Galatians 5: flesh and fruits

Know the difference between flesh and Spirit. The flesh wars against the Spirit; the Spirit wars against the flesh. (Galatians 5:17; Matthew 26:4) Are you feeding your flesh or your Spirit? (Galatians. 6:8; 1 Peter 2:12)

Have you left you past in your past? God will not introduce you to your Kingdom spouse until you allow Him to purge you from all uncleanness and ungodliness, and remove all those skeletons from your closet.

Have you divorced your previous spouse(s) in the Courts of Heaven? God is the Judge of Judges. He is the Just Judge. You may not have legally married that person, but you have sexual soul ties with him/her. Ask God to divorce you from that person(s). You are not married by Biblical standards.

You cannot take other people into your marriage, especially not a Kingdom Covenant. God will not allow it. There is no shame. There is no more condemnation in Christ Jesus. (Romans 8:1) Old things are passed away; behold all things are new. (2 Corinthians 5:14-21)

Repent. Pray. Get delivered. Get healed. Speak the Word of God over your life. Declare things that are not as though they were. (Genesis 17:5; Romans 4:16-22)

I don't know about you, but there are days where I need God the Father, God the Son, and God the Holy Ghost.

I needed to understand who and whose I am and my purpose in God. I have to be a whole, healed woman to become the Bride of Christ and wife in the earth, and for the Kingdom. The same discipline and principles apply to both. I am the Church in God's house and my house.

I cannot, I dare not love my husband with my flesh. That's not Kingdom. That's the world. In this flesh is no good thing. I will seek my husband in the Spirit and it will manifest in the natural. I choose to be his Aaron and Ur when necessary. I choose to war in the Spirit against every ungodly attack. I choose to speak life, love, joy, peace, and strength, and will see it manifest in the natural. I choose to love him unconditionally, sacrificially, intentionally, purposefully, on purpose. This is not about my feelings. Feelings are fickle. Feelings are temporary. I choose to pray before speaking or taking action on anything; even if it's from my husband. I will choose to hug him. Pray for him. I will not respond in kind. That old saying, "two wrongs don't make a right." I'll choose to pray. Forgive. That's a MUST. I will NOT give the enemy an opening. The Proverb 31 wife got up while her husband and children were sleep and sought God.

Early in the journey of consecration, I was blessed with following and learning from

Drs. Mike and DeeDee Freeman, Marriage Made E-Z. They taught from the word of God and with their testimony. Kingdom Covenant should be taught as God intended. Covenant is an Agreement between God and us, so how can we not teach it? It still stands today; my people perish for a lack of knowledge. Our

Pastors should be teaching and exemplifying and parents should be the main example of marriage God's way.

Dating...

Dating is you looking. God didn't tell us to go out looking. He who finds a wife finds a good thing and receives favor from the Lord. Adam didn't go looking for Eve. God created Eve for Adam. He found her when God presented her to him. We don't choose God. God calls us. Our Father chooses the Bride for the Bridegroom. God already knows who is for who because He knows what He put in each of us for His purpose. He knows our hearts. We get the benefits. When we're out looking, dating, do we truly know what or who we're looking for? We have lists, preferences, non-negotiables, and so on and so forth. What does that have to do with the Kingdom of God? Do you know who you are? Do you know what's in you? Do you know your purpose? Do you think your job, career, or work is your purpose? Are you passionate about what you do? Are you called to what you do? Do you know what's in you? How do you know what you're looking for? Will you know when you find her? Will you know when you meet him? Can you or would you declare, "this is now bone of my bones, flesh of my flesh?" Keep in mind, the man declares that, not the woman. The husband should be looking at a mirror reflection of himself, his purpose.

If you don't know who you are, your purpose then how do you know what you're looking for?

Where are you, Adam? Eve, get away from that tree.

Is it your spirit man looking or are you being led by your flesh? Covenant is Kingdom. Those who worship God must worship Him in Spirit and in Truth, not flesh. Flesh must be crucified daily. Flesh is your sin nature. Marriage does not correct what your flesh chose, it amplifies it more.

You have all these flesh marriages out there that grieves your spirit man, that you tied your spirit man to, and wonder why the next relationship didn't work out. You've been committing adultery over and over again. You're like a polygamist.

Dangers of dating....

While campaigning with my daughter, we were able to celebrate with our senior

Chapter 7 | Consecrate For Covenant

citizens New Year's Eve 2022. A few people came together to bless the seniors with a meal, food, and clothing donations. The Holy Ghost told me I would be asked to do a Bible Study. I connected with the gentleman that asked me if I would do a Bible Study. He gave me his name and number.

Fast forward after a few telephone conversations, I agreed to have lunch with him.

We're at lunch and he began to describe what he saw and thought about me, both physically and spiritually. The conversation continued when I took him back home.

The next time I'd see him was to take him to the bank, then we sat in front of the apartment building (senior high-rise) where he lived and talked for another hour or so. Again, he would describe me physically and spiritually. He said to me that he didn't know if our connection was spiritual or romantic. He decided it was spiritual and that I make him want to get back into Church. I told him that I am consecrated for my husband. While he was talking, I felt what I can only describe as a lust demon touching me. I recognized it and rebuked it immediately. I felt like I needed to take a shower as soon as I got home. That demon that's still on him tried to overtake me, come on me.

People can transfer spirits to you. That's why you must be careful who you talk to, go to lunch with, even though it's innocent. Stay in prayer, otherwise, you'll pick up other people's spirits. Those demon spirits will try to convince you it was an attraction and you'll end up in a relationship you should never have entertained.

It was insulting, that spirit. I appreciated his honesty. That spirit wasn't going home with me. That's the danger in dating someone that's not your husband or wife.

There wasn't any romantic interest on my part. Based on our conversations, he was still lustful; and that lust demon solidified, confirmed it. This is why dating someone who is not your husband/wife is dangerous…spiritually. You and I are constantly in spiritual warfare. The enemy is a liar. He is here to steal, kill, and destroy. Period.

How can I consecrate for Kingdom Covenant marriage if I'm dating?

God arranges marriages. For example:

When Abraham's wife Sarah died, and Isaac was 40 y.o., Abraham called his most trusted servant to find a wife for Issac. (Genesis 24). He had him swear not to look upon any of the Ites; Hittite, Jebuzite, etc. So, Abraham's most trusted servant as well as other servants packed camels and started on their journey. They stop at a well and Abraham's most trust servant gets off his camel and begins to pray to the God of his master, and was specific as to the type of woman. He asked for a woman with a serving heart, essentially. Yet God already had Isaac's wife picked out. As he was praying, a woman walks to the well to draw water and goes above and beyond what he requested. He then gave her gifts and asked for her father. Afterwards, they gathered to have a meal together. Abraham's most trusted servant told him why he was there and who sent him.

Abraham's most trusted servant's name was Eliezer; Rebekah was the woman who came to the well and did as Eliezer prayed for and more; Bethuel is the name of Rebekah's father. Eliezer means God's divine help or God is my help. Rebekah means to tie to, captivating beauty. Bethuel means house of God. So, Abraham sent God's divine help to the house of God to find a wife for Isaac.

Father God has chosen a Bride for His Son, Jesus. She will be presented to Him at the marriage supper of the Lamb dressed in linen without spot or blemish - a glorious Bride. She will rule and reign with her Bridegroom.

He who finds a wife, finds a good thing, and receives favor of the Lord.

God did not tell us to go looking in the hedges, highways, byways, bars, clubs, or His houses for a husband or wife. When our Mother was presented to our Father, our Father declared, "bone of my bones, flesh of my flesh." He recognized his rib.

God prepares the husband to receive his wife. God gave our Father (Adam) purpose, responsibility before creating our Mother (Eve) for him. Then he had a reason for his purpose. God gave our Father provision - a place to live and food to eat - before giving him his wife.

God is raising up Kingdom couples.

Everyone is not going to hear and see the same way because we're not all the same. It depends on how you spend time with God, it depends on what you're doing and where you go. How are you doing life? Do you read and listen to the word of God? Who are you listening to? Do you take classes, enroll in courses? Do you attend conferences? God speaks to you based on how you're listening.

The same way I hear from and listen to God is the same way I got to know my husband; and will continue. God knew I was watching and listening. You cannot pray for someone or something you don't know. I cannot intercede for someone or something I don't know.

God told us who we are and gave us purpose from the Beginning – Genesis.

The two people who God created were two whole people. They were created to reign in the earth together. They were created to subdue the earth together. They were created to take dominion over creation together. That has not changed. What had changed is that we live in a fallen world full of sin, darkness, and wickedness. Hence, we must be born again; so when we subdue and take dominion, we do it in Kingdom Authority. In the name of Jesus, I'm going to subdue and have dominion over this territory. The Lord will give me wherever my feet tread; as far as I can see and walk, just as God told Abraham. Today, I can drive and take an airplane, take flight. I can mount up on wings as an eagle.

Jesus said greater things will you do. We are to take territory and bring the territory into Kingdom order. There wasn't any sin in the garden of Eden. It was in Kingdom order. Our parents and the animals were in that garden together. Both people and animals ate plants. There weren't any carnivores.

When I trained in martial arts, it was about discipline, self-control, bringing the whole person together; body, soul and spirit, into alignment.

The Word of God is about aligning body, soul, and spirit with the Kingdom of God.

It's a discipline called faith.

In martial arts, you had to believe you could do certain things.

In Christianity, you must believe you can do all things through Christ who strengthens you. You must believe God will do what He said He would do and that He can in you and through you.

The two whole people in the garden walked and talked with God in the Garden. They heard God's voice walking in the Garden. We have the Holy Ghost to dwell with and walk and talk with all day, any day, every day. When our parents clothed themselves with fig leaves to cover the shame of their nakedness, the fig leaves eventually dried up and died because they were removed from their vine, their life source.

Jesus is the vine and we are to get connected by receiving Him as our savior, making Him Lord, and remaining connected. He said we are the branches and we are expected to grow fruit. Otherwise, those branches will be removed, fall off, and die. Those branches get thrown into fire to be burned.

Our Father is a loving and caring gardener, the husbandman, that prunes us so we can bear more fruit. In order to do that, we must grow. We will create a family tree from two strong, born-again branches. It takes faith just the size of a mustard seed. A great harvest comes out of a seed. It has to be watered and pruned with the word of God by the husbandman, our Father.

God knows each and every one of us. We can put on fig leaves all we want and try to hide thinking He doesn't know where we are. I guess those leaves were supposed to be like camouflage hiding amongst the trees. A psalmist said it like this, if I make my bed in hell, You are there. (Psalm 139)

I had to take my hand off God's hand, trying to prophesy how I was going to meet, to be introduced to my husband. I was all in God's business, calling it prophesying.

So, one day I stepped back and focused on what I needed to focus on. I continued to pray for him, his family, and the ministry he was charged with leading.

That focus shifted to my assignment, which was preparation for where I was going next. I couldn't shift because of a stalemate, an impasse. At the same time, taking care of my first ministry, my family. There are generations on my shoulders. There are three generations in my home at all times, and at times, four generations. My decisions would affect the generations in the earth and not yet in the earth.

There's one that God chooses to shift the direction of generations, of nations You need to disciple and they need to be prepared.

Conversations with My Husband

Chapter 8

Chapter 8 | Conversations with My Husband

Husband: *My parents have been married for 50 plus years. I'm divorced. I have been divorced several years now. I did not try to emulate what my parents have. I did the total opposite. I was Jonah for real.*

Me: My parents were together 20 plus years as "common law". They were married but estranged.

Husband: Okay. I'm divorced. Though my parents modeled and still do, a godly marriage, I did not. I saw it but I didn't know how they did it.

Me: My parents relationship was just the opposite. My Dad functioned, but not fully, because of his past relationship with his Dad. My Mom did not witness a godly marriage either, though her father was a Pastor. He stepped down because of the decisions he made. I'm a 3rd generation Preacher.

Husband: I'm a 4th generation Preacher. I was running from this wholeheartedly.

Me: God has a sense of humor for real.

Husband: (laughs) God absolutely has a sense of humor. This certainly was not my plan.

Me: I was trying to open a business. Called into ministry wasn't in my preview at all.

Husband: I had a lot of healing to do. A lot of understanding to get on how God sees marriage. I looked at my failures in relationship, especially my marriage. I can read what the word of God says, but how to do it was the disconnect.

Me: I understand. I'm divorced as well. That was not a godly marriage. God wasn't even invited, yet we were married in Church by a Pastor. I didn't have a relationship with God, so I didn't know He needed to be a huge part of marriage. I didn't even know God created marriage, let alone why He created Covenant.

Husband: I knew all of that and still didn't do it God's way. My relationship with God must be at a more intimate level, so our relationship will be at a level of intimacy where the enemy, including me, won't have a chance to get in to steal, kill, and destroy. I have children, you have children. So, what would they see in our marriage?

Me: We shouldn't just show them, for example, we should also tell them and teach them how. Just as you said, you saw your parents in a godly marriage and still do, yet you didn't know how. I watch family shows with married couples with children, yet there was no mention of God, as I think about it. The most was perhaps saying grace over a meal.

Husband: Wow. I don't recall that either. However, I had that growing up. Prayer with my now ex-wife wasn't consistent, except on Sundays and Bible Study. My prayer life needed significant improvement, as I said a higher level of intimacy with God.

Me: Prayer changes things, should not be just a Church cliché. I know prayer changes things. I know having an intimate relationship with God changes things, people, and places. Jesus needs to be Lord, not only Savior. We must make sure our children see that and know for themselves. And it's not for Sundays and Bible Study only. Prayer is the very foundation of life. It's the glue, so to speak, that holds everything together. Unless the Lord builds the house, it's builders labor in vain. Jesus is the chief cornerstone.

Husband: Wow. That's good. I don't think I ever heard that scripture applied to marriage. I've only ever heard it applied to the Church.

Me: Are we not the Church? Wherever we go there we are.

Husband: True. The Church is not a building. It's a body of people. The Body of Christ. I'm going to set that right there.

Me: That would take this conversation in a different direction. Let's stay in this vein.

Husband: Absolutely. I still have healing to do as a man, to be the best husband with God's help. I did the outward show, but inside was still not right. I've chosen relationships based on my flesh, then when they didn't work out it was the devil, and not me. I look forward to our prayers together daily. How you speak into me is not what I ever had before. I can feel God touch those areas I hid from everyone. People look at the outward appearance, but God through you speaks to my very soul. I even feel different. I can feel the healing I didn't realize I truly needed.

Me: It is a privilege to be able to see you and an honor to speak to your soul. With God's guidance and His wisdom, I choose to speak life into the husband God has called, chosen, and graced me for. I see the outward appearance. I'm not blind, yet I'm concerned that your soul looks better, and prospers. These bodies grow old, so if that's what attracts me to you only, what then in 20 years?

Husband: Wow. So true. This is the level of intimacy I've been missing. I want to be naked and unashamed with you. As we grow more intimate in our walk together, I want to be that safe place, space for you. I see you're comfortable talking to me, yet I see you're holding back some. I understand. We're both in a foreign space right now. God called, chose, and graced you to be my wife, as He called, chose, and graced me to be your husband. As we talk this journey together, we'll see why God called you for me and me for you. We have just only scratched the surface. I already see that you have experience, expertise in the things God gave me vision for, so I cannot wait to go even deeper.

Me: My Lord. This is certainly a "I've never been here before" space, place. As you said, we have only just scratched the surface. I really enjoy our prayer time together. Thank you for the life-giving words you speak to me. I treasure that time the most. God knows me intimately. He loves me with all the evidence. Our intimacy is growing as we pray and spend time together on purpose, intentionally.

Husband: Amen. I pray that our children see the love, respect, and honor in our relationship in words and deeds.

Me: Amen.

Imparting Into My Husband

I speak to God's Son
I speak to my Husband
I speak to the Dad
I speak to the Man
I speak to the Preacher
I decree, I declare, I intercede, I go to war.

Who I am speaking to, meaning, what he is going through at any moment, would be my focus. At the same time, not ignoring those parts of him. The whole man needs love, strength, peace, rest, joy, lifting up, talked off the ledge, tenderness.

I can speak into my husband because I was called, chosen, graced, and equipped.

Lord, I am speaking to Your son. First of all, you are God's child; His precious son. You are made in the image and after the likeness of God. You are His masterpiece. You are His workmanship. You are the apple of His eye. I speak to the unbelief. You are who God says you are, not your unbelief, not those insecurities you don't speak about. You are not your choices, your decisions. You are God's son. And He is pleased with you. Lord, strengthen him; bless him abundantly above all he can think or ask. I speak peace into his soul, his spirit. I speak joy unspeakable into his soul, his spirit. I speak Your wisdom, Lord, into his soul, his spirit. He is so precious in Your eyes. You know every intimate detail of him, from the crown of his head to the souls of his feet. Lord, what You are doing in him and through him is limitless, without boundaries. He is royalty. He is Your son and no one can snatch him away from You, Lord. He is Yours. And You are his. Resources will be no issue because he seeks and trusts in the source. He will know and see how much You love him like never before because You are doing a new thing in him and through him. You will be stronger, wiser, and wealthy with multiple streams of income. No more limits. All things are possible because you believe the God of your salvation. Stand still and God will fight your battles. Take your foot off the brakes.

I speak to my husband

My love, I see you. I see past that outward appearance. You are safe with me. I will not betray you. I honor you. I respect you. I adore you. I desire for you to love me and never let me go. My desire will only be for you, my husband. I will not look to the left or to the right. I need you to lead me. I want you to lead me. I desire for you to lead me. I submit my will to you. I choose to submit my will to you. I want to submit my will to you. Be strong. Be vigilant. Be courageous. Be wise. Be gentle. Be thoughtful. You are my covering. I am your wife; your wife only. I need your patience. I need grace as we navigate this mission called Covenant together. I was called, chosen and graced for you, to be your wife, no one else's, yours. This is a God thing.

I speak to Dad

I speak wisdom, patience, insight, foresight, resources, financial resources, and multiple streams of income. I speak legacy builder. I speak kinsmen redeemer. This is husband and Dad. You will put your hands on so much income that it will be more than enough for generations in the earth and generations to come. God will make your name great in the earth and heaven.

This segways into Pastor, Preacher, Husbandman

I speak strength for this leg of your journey. I speak wisdom, peace, joy, patience, a new birth, and debt free.

There's a great harvest of souls. Fresh oil flowing from the crown of your head to the hem of your garments. New territory for the Kingdom of God.

For the Businessmen

New territory – countries.
Legacy

Son, Brother, Uncle, Cousin, Friend

I speak patience, kindness, love, joy, honor, and respect.
Legacy.
Kinsmen Redeemer.
Thoughtfulness, insight.

God is going to blow your mind. Take off the limits.

When I speak into and to my husband, he is God's son first and always, and whatever mindset he is in at that time. His mindset could be on husband, dad, preacher, pastor, teacher, businessman, son, brother, uncle, or friend. I will know based on what comes out of his mouth.

God is a multi-faceted God. I am that I am. El Shaddai, Jehovah Tsidkenu, T'Sur, Shammah, Rapha, Jireh, Nissi, Shalom, M'Kaddesh, Way Maker, Miracle Worker. Battle Ax, Yeshua, the Lily of the Valley, the Rose of Sharon, the Bright and Morning Star, Alpha and Omega, King of Glory, Master, Savior, Lord. He is all those things to us and more.

We are made in His image and after His likeness, so we are multi-faceted.

www.ingramcontent.com/pod-product-compliance
Lightning Source LLC
Chambersburg PA
CBHW070331230426
43663CB00011B/2281